THE SACRED COOKBOOK

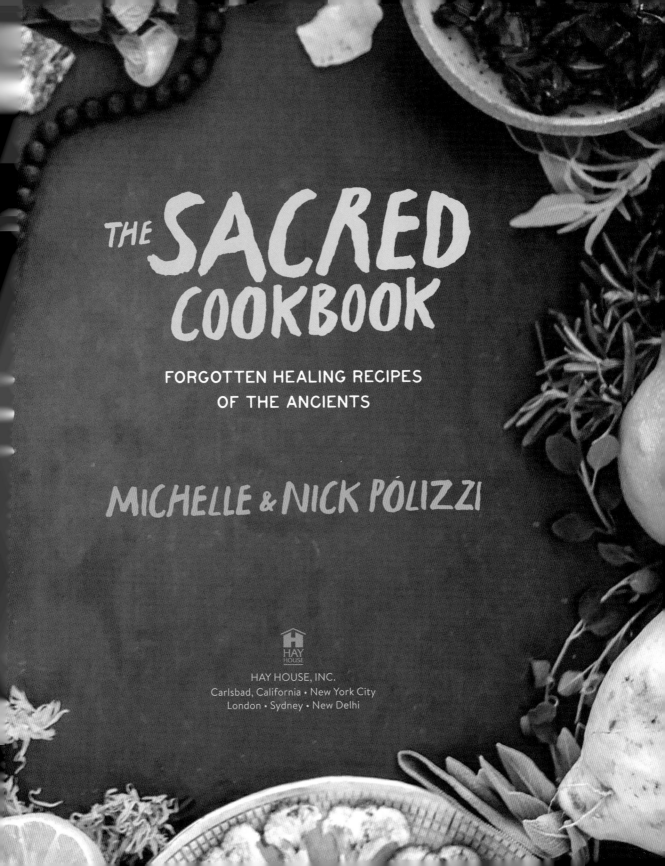

THE SACRED COOKBOOK

FORGOTTEN HEALING RECIPES
OF THE ANCIENTS

MICHELLE & NICK POLIZZI

HAY
HOUSE

HAY HOUSE, INC.
Carlsbad, California • New York City
London • Sydney • New Delhi

Copyright © 2023 by Nick Polizzi

Published in the United States by: Hay House, Inc.:
www.hayhouse.com® • **Published in Australia by:** Hay House
Australia Pty. Ltd.: www.hayhouse.com.au • **Published in the
United Kingdom by:** Hay House UK, Ltd.: www.hayhouse.co.uk
• **Published in India by:** Hay House Publishers India:
www.hayhouse.co.in

Cover design: Michelle Polizzi • *Interior design:* Shubhani Sarkar •
Interior photos/illustrations: Michelle Polizzi

Cataloging-in-Publication Data is on file at the Library of Congress

Hardcover ISBN: 978-1-4019-7351-3
E-book ISBN: 978-1-4019-7352-0

10 9 8 7 6 5 4 3 2

1st edition, October 2023

Printed in China

To the generations of cooks and herbalists
(women) who passed these recipes
forward through the centuries.
Without you, these sacred dishes
would be lost in the sands of time.

CONTENTS

INTRODUCTION: FOOD HEALS 1

LEAVES OF GRACE

Seaweed Salad 14

Mustard Greens Bhutuwa 17

Ginger Spinach. 18

Nigerian Bitter Leaf Stew (Ofe Onugbu) 20

Greens in Groundnut Sauce 23

Summer Chicory Salad 24

Mediterranean Kale Salad 27

Roasted Cauliflower Steaks 28

Saag Paneer. 30

Escarole Linguini. 33

MAJESTIC MUSHROOMS

Forest Porcini and Farro 39

Simple Chanterelle Mushrooms 43

Sautéed Morels with Elderflower
and Miner's Lettuce 44

Garlic Mushroom Dandelion Greens 47

Three Mushroom Stir-Fry 48

Duxelles 51

Mushroom Tapenade. 52

SOUPS AND STEWS FOR THE SOUL

Folk Healing Soup. 56

Savory Seaweed Broth 58

Traditional Berber Tagine 61

Medicinal Yellow Curry 62

Savory Winter Lentil Soup 65

Nourishing Bone Broth 66

Irish Brotchan Roy Foltchep Soup 69

Traditional Māori Puha Boil Up 70

Amerindian Pepperpot 73

Tom Yum Soup 74

TINY WONDERS (LEGUMES, SEEDS, AND NUTS)

Inca Quinoa Salad 78

Fertile Crescent Falafel. 81

Pine Nut Pilaf. 82

Comfort Khichdi with Tomato Onion Salad . . . 85

Lemon Quinoa Salad with Hemp Seed. 89

Arabian Hummus 90

BURIED TREASURES

Summer Borscht. 94

Roasted Winter Roots 97

Q'ero Potato Salad 98

Egyptian Lotus Root Salad 101

Quechua Yucca Salad 102

Oven-Roasted Herb French Fries. 105

GODLY GRAINS

Sasqu (Date Porridge) 108

Jungle Oatmeal 111

Kamut Berry Salad 112

Plant-Infused Polenta with Mushroom Medley . . 115
Asparagus Risotto. 118
Choctaw Cornbread 121
Sourdough Bread 122
Essene Sprouted Wheat Manna Bread 126
Roman Honey Cake 129

MASTERS OF WATER AND AIR

Al Kabsa 132
Fire-Roasted Chicken with Maya Adobo Sauce . 135
Quechua Ceviche. 138
Patarashca (Amazon Roasted Fish) 141
Nourishing Protein Patties 142
Ancient Herb-Marinated Chicken 145
Herbed Sausage 146
Medicinal Chinese Dumplings 149

DRIED AND CURED WITH CARE

Cree Pemmican 156
Aztec Granola Bars 158
Tarahumara Energy Bar 161
Bean, Seed, and Herb Crackers 162
Cacao Bites 165
Oven-Dried Kale Chips 166
Timeless Trail Mix 169

BITTER, BRINY, AND BOLD

Sacred Sauerkraut 172
Korean Kimchi 175
The Mesopotamian Pickle 178
Yogurt (Laban) 180
Superfood Yogurt Bowl. 181
Ethiopian Injera 183
Herbal Kombucha 184
Shamanic Fire Cider 187
Celtic Druids Honey Mead. 188

ENCHANTING SPICES AND SAUCES

Berbere Spice 192
Garam Masala 195
Nam Prik Pau 196
Heal-All Garlic and Olive Oil Infusion 199
Ha Sikil Pa'ak 202
Dandelion Pesto with Pine Nuts 204
Chimichurri 207
Tzatziki Sauce 208
Fennel Syrup 211
Honey Dijon Dressing 212
Spicy Herbal Honey 215
Moraba 'Yeh Anjir (Black Fig Jam) 216

TIME-TESTED TEAS AND TONICS

Reishi Tea 220
Holy Basil Elixir. 223
Homemade Coconut Milk 224
Tibetan Rhodiola Tea. 226
Pine Pollen Tea. 229
Mayan Hot Chocolate 230
Herbal Coffee Alternative 233
Oatstraw Infusion. 234
Holiday Mulled Wine. 237
Four-Herb Brain-Booster Tea 238
Maitake Chai 241
Chaga Latte Elixir 242
Ayurvedic Immune Booster 245
Ashwagandha Milk 246
Morning Maca Elixir 249
Ginger Intention Tonic 250

METRIC CONVERSION CHART 255
ENDNOTES 257
INDEX 265
ACKNOWLEDGMENTS 273
ABOUT THE AUTHORS 275

FOOD HEALS

Food is, and always has been, medicine. It nourishes every aspect of who we are, and nearly every ancient civilization around the world knew this to be true. For more than two decades, I've traveled to the ends of the earth, from hard-to-reach jungle regions of the Amazon to Bedouin encampments in the Sahara Desert, learning from remote cultures and documenting their unique pharmacopoeia of local herbals and traditional healing arts. From herbalists, midwives, grandmothers, and shamans, I've learned how to use local spices, herbs, and other ingredients to help heal the mind, body, and soul.

I know firsthand how much of an impact intentional eating can have on your healing journey. In my early 20s, I was diagnosed with a serious illness that modern medicine couldn't treat. I tried everything that my doctors and neurologists suggested, yet nothing worked. With conventional medicine offering me no solutions, I turned to natural remedies, which put me on the path of herbalism and what I fondly like to call "the people's medicine." I healed my body using these ancient practices, which included food.

My "unexplainable" recovery inspired me to dedicate my life and career to exploring ancient healing traditions and sharing this knowledge and wisdom with those who are also trying to ease their suffering, restore their health, and find a deeper connection to the world around them. I've spent almost two decades making documentary films and producing countless courses and workshops with the world's most sought-after healers and herbal wisdom keepers, including Rosemary Gladstar, considered to be the godmother of American herbalism; Tieraona Low Dog, M.D., legendary wise woman, professor, and natural healer; and Sandra Ingerman, the most renowned living shamanic practitioner. I'm also the founder of The Sacred Science, an online community devoted to bringing people deeper into the powerful healing practices of our ancestors.

It was during the initial research phase of my film *The Sacred Science* that I felt drawn to dig deeper into our ancient edible roots. With the intention of documenting an intact shamanic tradition, my production crew and I canvassed the globe, investigating a number of remote healing traditions dating back thousands of years. We would work late into the night, tracing the remnants of fading lineages back to their origins. Often we would hit a dead end—a single document or personal account being all that was left of what was once a prominent school of wisdom. But sometimes our long hours paid off, revealing a system or protocol that demonstrated incredible healing potential.

As we plunged further into the early periods of recorded human existence, we frequently came across references to particular herbs, spices, foods, and drinks that were held sacred by certain peoples. I was fascinated by how many healing spices and other potent ingredients were found in ancestral medicines *and* ancestral food.

So many culinary ingredients were not only delicious but held extraordinary health benefits. Which begged the question: What did our forebears prioritize most . . . flavor or medicine?

My mind thirsts for answers to questions like these: Why was so much oregano used in ancient Italian cuisine? Was it just because oregano tasted good, or was it because this aromatic herb has antimicrobial properties that can kill bacteria and other pathogens in meat?[1] Or perhaps because oregano is an effective natural antibiotic?[2]

Curry is another example. Is it by chance that the key ingredient, turmeric, is also one of the most anti-inflammatory compounds on the planet? Is it a coincidence that scientists now know that curcumin, the most active compound in turmeric, can only be made bioavailable if you combine it with a fat (and a specific type of black pepper)? And that ancient Indians just so happened to create a dish called curry, combining turmeric with coconut milk (one of the healthiest fats) and a healthy dose of the specific pepper that unlocks all the beneficial compounds in turmeric?

How did our ancestors know to prepare and combine certain ingredients into delicious meals that doubled as potent healing potions?

As I've trekked across the globe documenting and working with some of the world's foremost natural healers, I've taken extensive notes on the time-tested dishes from each tradition I've encountered. I've carefully logged the herbs, spices, and other ancient ingredients that are used, many of which have now been scientifically proven to have medicinal value.

Every step of this journey has been taken alongside my wife, Michelle, a brilliant artist and natural healer. She, too, is a seeker of ancient wisdom and someone who values ancestral medicines. Together we search for new ways to bridge the past with the present, co-creating a life for ourselves and our two sons that heals and empowers everyone. Like many parents, we are dedicated to choosing foods that will nourish our boys—physically and spiritually. And most important, these dishes have to taste amazing!

Michelle was the driving force behind this cookbook. She told me it was our responsibility to curate all the ancient recipes and healing ingredients we use in our house and share this knowledge with our fellow seekers on the natural medicine path. As the owner of her own design company, Lovely Day Design Studio, and the former art director for major entertainment companies like HBO, MTV, and BRAVO, Michelle is an accomplished photographer, designer, ceramicist, and illustrator who was kind enough to lend her creative genius to this book. All the images and illustrations that you're about to see in this cookbook came from her.

In keeping with her vision, the recipes you're about to discover combine the edible treasures we've brought back from ancient food traditions around the world. In deciding what dishes to include, Michelle and I used the following criteria:

1. Recipes or ingredients had to be traced back at least 500 years.
2. Every recipe had to be adaptable, as needed, for our modern world.
3. Herbs, spices, and other ingredients had to have medicinal properties backed by research and science.
4. The end result had to taste *delicious*.

FOOD IS SACRED

As much as food can help us treat and prevent physical ailments, there's also a spiritual component that comes from the food we choose to eat.

Food is truly sacred.

I learned this lesson as a boy. Some of my earliest and fondest memories were working in my mother's New England restaurant, Plain Jane's, where she was the chef/owner and a kindred spirit to local patrons. I don't know if you'd technically call it "working" when I was nine years old, learning how to dice tomatoes and move big blocks of cheese through an industrial cheese shredder, but it was certainly the start of a life of food reverence.

Although my mom was the creative force and lifeblood behind Plain Jane's, she actually learned to cook from my Italian grandparents. We'd spend entire weekends making delicious meals with Grandpa Nick and Grandma Fran, who eventually moved into an in-law apartment we built for them in our basement in Connecticut. My grandparents left us a handmade black book of traditional dishes from the old country that Michelle and I still turn to as we raise our two sons.

NOT REALLY PLAIN—Peggy Polizzi, one of the new owners of Plain Jane's restaurant, replenishes a tray of muffins for the breakfast crowd. Renovations at the restaurant include the opening of a new dining room which is also available for group functions.—Fran Sikorski photo.

Nick's mom holding a plate of muffins in the front kitchen of Plain Jane's, 1987.

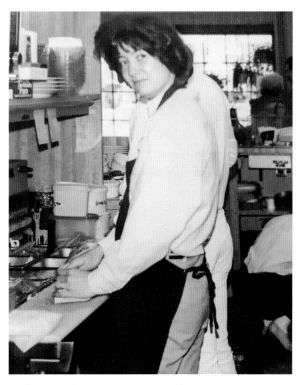

Nick's mom making one of her famous veggie pouches during a weekday lunch rush, 1988.

Nick's Italian grandparents, Nick Sr. and Fran.

Nick putting whipped cream on desserts at Plain Jane's, 1991.

Nick Sr. (my namesake) came from a long line of bakers. In the early 1900s, his father (my great-grandfather) started The Red Diamond Bakery in Brooklyn, New York, soon after he emigrated from Italy. My grandfather grew up sweating next to a gigantic industrial bread oven before he went to school, rising with his brothers at 2:30 every morning and often arriving at school an hour late. The Red Diamond was one of the oldest bakeries in Brooklyn until it was knocked down, along with many other local landmarks, to make way for the Brooklyn-Queens Expressway in the mid-1940s.

I can still vividly picture Grandpa Nick silently kneading dough in his kitchen like it was a prayer to the Almighty. Grandpa Nick never hurried. He was in his own world, not just working the ingredients but *feeling* into them.

My Grandma Fran approached cooking and preparing meals much as my grandfather did, but while he worked in silence, she treated the kitchen as a place to connect with her loved ones. She used time spent in the kitchen with my sister and me as a way to talk with us about life and what was going on in our worlds. It was community, communion, connection.

Cooking was love.

While I remember the food always tasted amazing, it was the energy my grandparents gave off that I can still feel more than 40 years later. Being in the kitchen with them was its own brew of unconditional love and acceptance. As bad as life seemed—whether I was in elementary, middle, or high school—I would come home and find my grandparents in their kitchen. And I knew everything would be okay.

The legendary Brooklyn apartment dinner table with a bunch of Nick's Italian aunts, uncles, and cousins. His grandma Fran is the dark-haired woman with red lipstick sitting fourth from the front on the left side of the table.

Sunday dinner with Nick's father, Steve (front left), brothers, sisters-in-law, and grandpa Nick Sr. standing in the background.

Their son Steve, my father, was the first person to give me full reign of the kitchen, teaching me how to make a traditional Italian tomato sauce when I was in 5th grade. He knew how much I wanted to cook Sunday dinner and actually let me take over the cooking responsibilities, which gave me the confidence that I could "do hard things well" at a time in my life when I really needed it. Love you, Pop.

The kitchen was, and still is, my sanctuary. It's like a campfire that I gather around with my friends, family, Michelle, and our sons to warm our hands and nourish our souls. That's the mystery and beauty of food. What we eat, how we prepare it, and who we share it with has the power to feed us on many levels.

What we choose to eat can help boost our energy, strengthen our immune system, lower inflammation, improve heart health and circulation, calm our nervous system, aid digestion, promote a healthy microbiome, and improve our memory, concentration, moods, and overall brain health.

Food also nourishes our spirits. The wise among us know that our kitchens are more than simply places to cook. They are sacred spaces where unique ingredients are transformed into delicious potions, brimming with health benefits. And it's through our kitchens and cooking that we can also connect more deeply with our ancestors, the natural world, and our friends, communities, and families.

Since childhood I've often been told, "You're just like your mother." It's been said with warm, knowing smiles by loving friends—and with exasperated sighs by those who don't get either of us. In any case, I consider it the ultimate flattery to be compared to the smartest, most empathetic, old-soul, no B.S. person I've ever met.

A former restaurateur (who did it at a time when it wasn't customary for a mother of two to reach for something bigger), my mother has always been an inspiration to me. I wanted to be creative like her, to make people smile like she does, and to have just an ounce of the world-weary Irish wit that she was somehow born with. I've always wanted to make her proud, not in any material success but by doing as she does. Living by the unwritten codes that can only be felt, not explained.

My mom was also instrumental in the creation of this book, helping me research and recreate many of the ancient recipes you're about to encounter. Without her *The Sacred Cookbook* would be just another exciting but unmanifested idea in my head. And it's a reminder of how food can bring us closer together.

Michelle and I hope these recipes inspire your curiosity as much as they have ours, that they make your culinary and cooking experiences that much richer and more sacred, and that they keep you and your loved ones healthy for generations to come. As you journey throughout these pages, may you find inspiration, joy, connection, and true medicine in the food you eat.

Stay curious.

THE SACRED COOKING PHILOSOPHY

Through The Sacred Science, my team and I have explored countless cultures, and despite their many differences, most share a sacred reverence for food—how it's prepared, served, and eaten. While modern life has largely removed the sacredness from food and eating, we have the power to restore it in our homes.

When we do, we honor our ancestors, connect to Mother Earth, reestablish our place in nature, fortify our bodies, and build strong bonds with the friends, families, and communities with whom we share our meals.

Over the years, I've developed four essential ingredients for sacred cooking. You can use these to kick-start your own rituals or to create new ones. If you're cooking with kids, these practices can be a terrific way to get small humans involved while opening the floodgates of deeper connection with them. These sacred practices can also help teach your children to develop healthy and wholehearted connections to their food.

FOUR ESSENTIAL INGREDIENTS OF SACRED COOKING

1. MAKE YOUR KITCHEN A SACRED SPACE.

Grandpa Nick was the keeper of our family's cooking tradition, so he instilled in me a deep reverence for food and all its delicious magic. My grandfather's meticulous way of preparing the ingredients, cooking each dish, and cleaning up while he went along was a moving meditation.

I used to get tingles up my spine just watching as he and my grandmother prepared the homemade manicotti, the white bean and escarole soup, and the pulpo salad with fresh octopus. Grandpa Nick would lick his upper lip— an indicator that he was really concentrating on a difficult maneuver—while tucking the semolina dough under a delicately positioned ravioli. Each moment in the kitchen felt so rich, so tranquil, so filled with intention, meaning, and joy. The way life should be.

My father still tells stories about the old days: Sunday night dinners with all his cousins, aunts, and uncles crowded around a huge dinner table, crammed into a tiny Brooklyn dining room, and how this was "where it all happened." This was where stories of the old country were told, where my dad witnessed my grandfather's fluid banter with his uncles and my grandmother's playful gossip with her sisters. One big family melting pot, where everyone was noticed and loved. And, of course, the food was delicious.

We have the power to create a similar sacred space in our kitchens for ourselves, our families, and our friends. Whether we spend 10 minutes or two hours in the kitchen, it can always be a portal to connecting. You don't have to buy any fancy equipment or decorate your kitchen in a certain way. It's about the *intentions* you bring with you when you step into the kitchen. See your kitchen for the sacred space that it is, and so it will become.

DOES EATING ORGANIC MATTER?

Whether we should eat organic is one of the hottest debates in health and wellness circles. Clearly, our ancestors didn't use chemicals and pesticides to grow and raise their food. So if you want to limit your exposure to substances from a lab, then opting for organic is the way to go, assuming that it fits your budget and lifestyle and is accessible for you and your family. If organic doesn't work, for whatever reason, then it's okay! Please, let go of any stress around eating organic. These recipes focus on nourishing our families with fresh fruits and vegetables, whole grains, minimally processed foods, natural sweeteners, and moderate animal-protein sources.

2. CONNECT TO SEASONAL EATING.

Modern life has brought with it many extraordinary innovations and transportation marvels, one of which is that in colder climates we can eat strawberries in January, pears in the spring, or asparagus in October. Walk into any grocery store, and it's understandable if you believe all foods are available in every season.

But rewind time and that wasn't the story. Our ancestors ate seasonally, largely because they didn't have a choice. Lettuce and leafy greens, tomatoes, and corn were available in the summer. They'd harvest to eat and store apples, potatoes, squashes, and other root vegetables in the fall to help get them through the harsh winter months. In the spring people would find asparagus, garlic, peas, and cauliflower.

Although we're graced by such abundance of choice and variety at all times throughout the year, there is still something invaluable to eating what's grown seasonally in your area. Eating seasonally is an invitation for you to connect more deeply to the natural environment and the natural life cycles surrounding you and the place you call home. Cycles of life and death, of sowing seeds and reaping harvests, govern our world—whether we're conscious of them or not. When you eat seasonally, you return to the cycle of life. And it becomes a portal into the great mystery that governs our world and confounds and inspires us.

Seasonal foods also usually taste better! They're fresher and more filled with life. The farther food has to travel, the earlier it has to be picked. A plump, juicy orange can't be harvested at its prime, when it's most lush and delicious— otherwise it would spoil in transit from Florida to Wisconsin.

Eating seasonally is not all or nothing. I invite you to play with it and have fun. Start learning about the local farms in your area. Visit local farmers markets or co-ops, and seek out opportunities to research and discover what foods grow when in your area. Then try to incorporate them into your meals once or twice a week. If that doesn't work, then try every other week or once a month.

When we eat the food grown near our homes, it also creates a deeper, richer connection between us and our environment. And that is a profound gift unto itself.

3. EMBRACE CURIOSITY, EXPLORING THE STORY OF AN INGREDIENT.

Creating healing, restorative foods can be about more than following a recipe word for word. It's another invitation to explore the unique story and character of your ingredients. Just like each of us, everything you eat has a story that can be traced back hundreds, sometimes thousands of years.

Take the herb thyme. It's native to southern Europe, and the word comes from the Greek word *thymos*, meaning "to fumigate." Is it any wonder, then, that in ancient Greek temples, thyme was burned as incense? Ancient Romans bathed in thyme to increase their courage, and this fragrant herb was used medicinally to help open bronchial passages and heal coughs.

Learning the lineage of an ingredient is also a way to experience deep reverence for the foods we eat, for the small life forces that allow us to go on living, breathing, and experiencing this world.

When we trace the history and learn the story of an ingredient, it can help us tune in to the subtle energies found in what we eat. Most indigenous societies around the world

communicate with plants—it's part of plant medicine. It's believed that plants and humans can communicate, and the plant will tell wise ones how it can best be used, whether now is the right time to harvest, and how much to take. In return, wise ones will offer prayers of thanks, and they will enter into spaces of deep respect, honoring the grandmother plants for medicine and food.

While our culture has largely lost these ways of living in accord with the natural world, we can learn them. We can honor our food by understanding their stories, connecting to their pasts, and honoring the present and the gift of life they bestow upon us.

This is an invitation to research and learn more about the origins of your food. Discover where it's originally from, the origins of its name, how it was used medicinally, what recipes it was used in, and where it traveled.

The deeper you delve in learning about the dishes you're creating and the ingredients you're consuming, the richer your connection becomes to your food and the natural world itself.

4. BLESS YOUR FOOD.

To our ancestors, sustenance meant far more than satisfying one's appetite. Many considered these morsels to be a sacred gift from the Divine, every bite laden with meaning.

The sacred "before-meal" prayer—offering thanks for the bounty and abundance that feed and nourish our bodies—can be found in most civilizations throughout the world. We still see remnants of this tradition in many modern religions like Christianity, where families will "say grace" before a meal, and in Judaism, where kosher foods are those blessed by a rabbi. Besides the religious connotations, blessing food has long been a grounding reminder, for even the smallest family members, of the importance of being grateful for what we have.

While Grandpa Nick's food bedazzled the taste buds, perhaps his greatest legacy and impact came before we even lifted our forks to our mouths. He said the most powerful grace I've ever heard. Lucid, devotional, inspirational, humble, vulnerable—an entranced conversation with God. Once the food was laid out and everyone was seated, Grandpa Nick would look around the table, making gentle eye contact with everyone. Then he'd reach for the hand of the person seated to his right and left, prompting them to do the same, until the circle was complete and connected.

My grandfather would then close his eyes, bow his head, and in a fast, rhythmic cadence pray to God to bless the food and shed his light and love on everyone at the table, before ending by expressing the deepest gratitude for the abundance that surrounded us.

This wasn't for show; it was communication.

When the blessing was complete, Grandpa Nick would open his eyes, lift his head, and with a sweet smile on his face, say, "Are you ready to eat?" And then we'd all dig in. He always served everyone else before himself.

I'm doing my best to follow my grandfather's example. In my family, Michelle and I have a "no devices at the dinner table" rule. Even on the nights when we don't make everything from scratch, we take the time to ponder the origin of our food and bless our meals for the sustenance they provide our bodies, minds, and spirits. I hope that my sons feel the sacredness of our food and that this practice will stay with them just as it's stayed with me. Carrying

on my grandfather's tradition is also a way for me to connect to him and to give my sons the chance to connect with their ancestors too.

Blessing your food before you eat doesn't have to be religious, although it certainly can be, depending on your beliefs. It's simply acknowledging the food you're about to consume, the plant or animal that has given its life force so that yours may continue. Blessing your food can be done aloud or silently. The blessing can be short or long. It's not what's said; it's about pouring your intention and feeling gratitude and grace for the beautiful wonders of life.

LEAVES of GRACE

Sometimes I wish I could photosynthesize so that just by being, just by shimmering at the meadow's edge or floating lazily on a pond, I could be doing the work of the world while standing silent in the sun.

— ROBIN WALL KIMMERER

Greens of all shapes and sizes have been readily consumed, traded, and even used in rituals for thousands of years. Kale, for example, was a prized cruciferous vegetable in ancient Greek and Roman markets, while spinach, known as the "Persian Green," has been a part of Middle Eastern cuisine for even longer. To many folks, especially in the United States, the term *collard greens* evokes images of Southern cooking, but this member of the cabbage family, originating in the eastern Mediterranean region and Asia Minor, dates back to prehistoric times. Historians believe that either the Romans or the Celts of northern Europe brought collard greens to Britain and France in 400 B.C.

Many of the foods mentioned in this cookbook have a sacred ritual or symbolism attached to them, and greens are no different. The greening of the fields and forests in spring has always been considered a sign of health and good tidings from Mother Nature. Our forefathers and ancestors knew early on that a generous helping of greens would bring about our own well-being, and good luck too. More specifically, the Egyptians and ancient Chinese connected green leaf lettuce to enhanced sexuality and reproduction. Interestingly, the Hebrew word for Swiss chard is almost identical to their word for "to throw out, or cause to disappear," and the green is ritually prepared to remove life challenges or adversities.

Travel to the Deep South in the U.S. and you'll hear folklore that hanging a fresh collard leaf above your front door will ward off evil. They say you can tell a true greens eater from the rest by inviting them into the kitchen while you cook up a nice batch of collards and black-eyed peas. According to this old wives' tale, the smell from this traditional dish is truly pungent and will scare off anyone with evil in their heart!

SEAWEED SALAD

Contributed by Rosemary Gladstar, considered to be the "godmother of American herbalism" and internationally renowned for her herbalism knowledge and stewardship. Learn more at the scienceandartofherbalism.com.

Seaweed is an ancient medicine and food that humans have turned to for thousands of years. Archaeologists have found evidence of nine different seaweed species at the Monte Verde site in Chile, dating back 13,980 to 14,220 years. Monte Verde is believed to be the oldest known human settlement in the Americas. Found along coastal regions throughout the world, seaweed was used to treat various ailments. The Romans used it on burns, rashes, and wounds, while traditional Chinese and Japanese medicines often make hot water extracts for cancer.

This recipe calls for either hiziki (sometimes spelled hijiki) or arame. Both are delicious, mild-flavored seaweeds. Hiziki is my personal favorite. It's mainly grown off the coasts of Korea, Japan, and China, and it has more calcium in 1 tablespoon than an 8-ounce glass of milk. It's also rich in fiber and iron. Arame is similar in flavor and grows on the West Coast. (If harvesting off the coast, be sure to clean and wash your seaweed thoroughly.) It, too, has iron and calcium, as well as lignan, which may have antioxidant effects.

This dish highlights the wonderful flavor of seaweed. Flavors are blended together by adding a hot, sweet, spicy, and pungent sauce. Traditionally served cold, this dish is also delicious hot.

2 onions, chopped

4 to 6 garlic cloves

1 to 2 tablespoons fresh grated ginger

2 cups thinly sliced carrots

1 package (2 ounces) hiziki or arame (dried)

4 cups cooked brown rice

½ cup low-sodium tamari

¼ cup honey

2 to 3 tablespoons toasted sesame seed oil (it must be toasted), divided

Cayenne, to taste

Sauté the onions in 1 tablespoon of sesame oil until golden brown. Add the garlic and ginger. Cook for a few minutes.

Add the carrots. Sprinkle them with a very small amount of water, just enough to keep ingredients from sticking or burning. Cover the pan and let steam over low heat.

In the meantime, prepare the seaweed. First, reconstitute it by soaking it in 1 to 2 cups of water for about 15 minutes, or until soft. Chop it into bite-size pieces. Drain the seaweed well.

When the carrots are soft, add the drained seaweed to the pot and cook for a few more minutes. You can add more seaweed if you like, depending on your personal taste.

Add the rice and stir well.

SAUCE

In a separate saucepan, warm the tamari, honey, sesame oil, and cayenne. The sauce should taste sweet, hot, spicy, and utterly delicious. Adjust the flavors to your liking.

Pour the sauce over the seaweed and rice mixture, stir, and serve.

MUSTARD GREENS BHUTUWA

SERVES 4

Many associate mustard (as a condiment) with Germany due to its famous hot dog pairing, but this leafy vegetable actually has its origins in the Himalayan mountains. Nepal is the birthplace of the mustard green, and during ancient times it was often carried along the spice trade roads between China, India, Europe, and Africa. In those days the plant was predominantly known for its seed, which was more easily transported than the fresh leaves.

Like most of the ingredients featured in this book, mustard greens are also extremely good for you. They can aid digestion,[1] lower cholesterol,[2] reduce inflammation,[3] and help stave off cancer.[4]

This dish pairs wonderfully with basmati rice.

- 3 tablespoons mustard seed oil or olive oil
- ½ teaspoon lovage seeds or 1½ tablespoons minced celery leaves
- 1 teaspoon Szechuan pepper or a pinch of coriander mixed with ground black pepper
- ½ teaspoon mustard seeds
- ½ teaspoon cumin seeds
- 1 tablespoon minced ginger
- ½ teaspoon ground black pepper
- 1 tablespoon minced garlic
- ¼ teaspoon ground turmeric
- 1½ teaspoons dried chili flakes
- 1 pound mustard greens, washed and chopped (or substitute with spinach)
- 1 teaspoon Himalayan sea salt
- Black pepper, to taste
- 2 tablespoons finely chopped fresh dill weed

Add the mustard seed oil to a large skillet over medium heat.

Add the lovage seeds, Szechuan pepper, mustard seeds, and cumin seeds and toast them until golden and fragrant.

Lower the heat and add the ginger, ground pepper, garlic, turmeric, and dried chili flakes and cook for another minute.

Add the mustard greens and continue to cook on low heat for 7 to 8 minutes until softened.

Add the salt and pepper to taste. Garnish with dill weed. Serve immediately.

NOTE: To give this dish a slightly more Thai flavor, try adding a teaspoon of coconut oil to each bowl as it is served.

GINGER SPINACH

SERVES 2

Indigenous to southern China, ginger has been used by healers to treat indigestion and joint pain for over 5,000 years. This spicy root continues to be an important ingredient in many Chinese medicines today. By the late first century A.D., ginger had spread to the Spice Islands and throughout all of Asia and Europe. Ginger was so highly valued in ancient Rome that a pound of it was equal in value to an entire sheep.

Exported primarily from India today, ginger is treasured around the world for its distinct flavor and aroma in cooking, as well as for its powerful medicinal properties. Ginger can be effective in settling stomach discomfort, including nausea,[5] and in reducing inflammation[6] and the pain and discomfort caused by osteoarthritis.[7]

2 tablespoons rice wine vinegar

2 teaspoons cornstarch

¼ teaspoon sea salt

1 tablespoon peanut oil

1 tablespoon fresh sliced ginger root

3 cloves garlic, sliced

4 cups spinach leaves

5 to 6 scallions, green and white parts, sliced diagonally

1 tablespoon sesame oil

1 teaspoon sesame seeds

In a small bowl, combine the vinegar, cornstarch, and salt and mix into a paste. Set the mixture aside.

Add the peanut oil to a large skillet over medium-high heat. When heated, sauté the ginger and garlic for 1 minute and then quickly add the spinach leaves and scallions. Cook until barely wilted.

Add the vinegar and cornstarch paste, and continue stirring until heated.

Drizzle with sesame oil and sprinkle with sesame seeds. Serve immediately.

NOTE: A great trick for storing fresh ginger is to peel it and keep it in the freezer in a sealed plastic bag. It's easy to grate while frozen, so you don't even need to thaw it.

NIGERIAN BITTER LEAF STEW (OFE ONUGBU)

SERVES 6

The bitter leaf, also called Onugbu, is one of the most widely used cooking vegetables in Africa. There is much debate about which particular tribe was the first to use this highly medicinal plant for culinary purposes, but most evidence points to the Igbo people of southeastern Nigeria as pioneers of this sacred food staple. The Igbos are said to be a spiritually advanced people who value the integrity of an individual far more than material wealth.

Published research is hard to find in North America, but within Nigeria, bitter leaf is a go-to household remedy for a variety of ailments and has been for thousands of years. From a medicinal perspective, bitter leaf is believed to help cleanse blood, and today researchers are studying whether bitter leaf could be a source for anticancer drugs.[8]

You will have to hunt to find bitter leaves in the United States or Europe. They are often available in dry form at Jamaican and African grocery stores and some health food stores, or you may find them online. If you can't find this fresh green, a great substitute is a combination of kale, turnip leaves, and dandelion greens.

- 8 taro, also called cocoyam, peeled and chopped into large chunks
- 1 bunch bitter leaf (or substitute with kale, turnip leaves, and dandelion greens washed and drained)
- 6 pieces cow tripe, cleaned and fat trimmed
- 1 pound dried unsalted codfish
- 1 pound stewing beef, cubed
- 3 cubes vegetable bouillon
- 1 cup dried and ground crayfish
- ½ cup red palm oil
- Sea salt and pepper, to taste

Fill a medium-sized pot with water and boil the taro. You will know the taro is done when it becomes soft and can be pierced with a fork.

Remove the taro and mash it in a bowl or with a mortar and pestle until it's thick and creamy.

Wash the bitter leaf until it is clean and, most important, there is no trace of bitterness left. If it is still bitter after washing, parboil it for 10 minutes and rinse, discarding the water.

In a large stockpot on high heat, add the cow tripe, dried codfish, and 5 cups of water and bring to a boil. Reduce to a simmer and cook until the tripe curls up on the edges.

Add the stewing beef and bouillon and cook until tender, approximately 1 hour.

Add the ground crayfish and bitter leaf. Stir and simmer for 10 more minutes (if you parboiled the bitter leaf, wait until the next step to add it).

(CONTINUED)

Drizzle the red palm oil on top. Next, dollop the mashed taro in chunks over the surface. Do not stir in these ingredients—you want the taro dollops to dissolve naturally.

Bring the soup to a boil and cook on medium heat for an additional 25 minutes. Once the soup has thickened to your desired texture, remove the excess taro chunks and discard them.

Season with salt and pepper to taste. Serve immediately.

GREENS IN GROUNDNUT SAUCE

SERVES 4

This Kenyan recipe, variations of which are found all over central and southern Africa, combines collard greens and kale with a common feature of African cuisine: the groundnut (or peanut). In Swahili, the word for greens is *Sukuma Wiki*, which means "stretch the week." In certain parts of Africa these greens grow like weeds and are often used to add inexpensive nutrition and necessary calories to the diet. Collard greens are also rich in potassium, fiber, and vitamins A, C, and K.

2 tablespoons peanut oil

1 onion, finely chopped

1 large bunch collard greens, stems removed and leaves chopped

1 large bunch kale, stems removed and leaves chopped

1 cup vegetable broth

1 ripe tomato, chopped (or a 15-ounce can diced tomato, drained)

½ cup peanut butter

Sea salt and cayenne pepper, to taste

¼ cup chopped peanuts

In a large skillet, heat the peanut oil over medium-high heat and lightly sauté the onion. Add the collard green and kale leaves. Sauté until brightly colored.

Add the broth and tomato and simmer for about 10 minutes.

In a separate bowl, add a ladle of hot broth from the pan to the peanut butter and whisk until smooth.

Add the peanut butter mixture to the skillet and simmer until heated. Add the sea salt and cayenne pepper to taste. Garnish with chopped peanuts and serve immediately.

NOTE: To add some more kick to this recipe, add 1 teaspoon of Berbere Spice (page 192).

SUMMER CHICORY SALAD

Chicory's medicinal and culinary roles can be traced back to ancient Egypt and Greece. While chicory leaves were regularly eaten in salads, its roots were believed to help heal jaundice, gout, and liver and gallbladder ailments. This endive is known as a popular coffee alternative that will also up your prebiotic intake.

Chicory leaves contain vitamins A and K, which are good for skin and bone health. Plus, this leafy green is high in vitamin C, which helps boost your immune system, and it contains essential B vitamins, giving you an energy kick. We've also added the dried red seaweed known as dulse, which grows in the cooler waters of the northwestern Pacific Ocean and the North Atlantic. It has been used as food and medicine for over 1,000 years. Dulse contains the minerals potassium and iodine, the latter of which can support the thyroid, helping regulate metabolism and energy.

2 tablespoons minced shallot

1 teaspoon Dijon mustard

1 tablespoon apple cider vinegar

Sea salt and freshly ground pepper, to taste

3 tablespoons olive oil

1 bunch chicory, roughly chopped

1 head escarole, chopped

1 head radicchio, chopped

4 tablespoons dried dulse

2 tablespoons raw pumpkin seeds

1 ounce parmesan cheese (for a vegan dish, substitute with nutritional yeast)

In a blender, pulse the shallot, mustard, and vinegar. Season with salt and pepper to taste. Pour the mixture into a small bowl and whisk in the oil in a slow stream to make a dressing.

Rinse and dry the chicory, escarole, and radicchio and toss them in a large salad bowl with the dressing.

Top with the dulse, raw pumpkin seeds, and parmesan. Serve immediately.

MEDITERRANEAN KALE SALAD

SERVES 4 TO 6

Native to the Mediterranean, kale is considered to be one of the most nutrient-dense foods on the planet. That's because when you eat this hearty green, you'll absorb vitamins A, K, C, and B_6 plus manganese, calcium, copper, potassium, and magnesium. When it comes to keeping your body healthy, kale should be a go-to. Recent studies suggest it contains properties that keep cancer at bay[9] and bind stomach acid, which can lower cholesterol,[10] and it has important flavonoids that reduce inflammation, lower blood pressure, and ward off viruses and depression.[11]

KALE SALAD

2 cups chopped kale

2 cups shredded red cabbage

2 cups chopped broccoli

2 carrots, shredded

1 bell pepper, diced

2 avocados, diced

½ cup chopped parsley

1 cup walnuts

1 tablespoon sesame seeds

LEMON-GARLIC DRESSING

½ cup lemon juice (about 2½ lemons)

½ cup olive oil

1 clove garlic, minced

1 teaspoon minced fresh ginger

1 teaspoon fresh rosemary leaves

1 teaspoon raw honey

A pinch of cayenne

1 tablespoon sea salt

In a large salad bowl, mix all the salad ingredients.

Process all the dressing ingredients in a medium blender until a creamy consistency is reached.

Add the dressing to the salad and toss to coat all the leaves with dressing. Serve immediately.

ROASTED CAULIFLOWER STEAKS

SERVES 6

Part of the cabbage family but the only member whose leaves aren't eaten, the cauliflower is said to have originated on the island of Cyprus before spreading to Syria, Turkey, Egypt, Italy, and Spain. This white, crunchy vegetable is actually a flower bud that hasn't flowered (same with broccoli). We can thank our ancient ancestors, who artificially selected and cultivated cauliflower from a wild mustard plant, for this versatile vegetable. But looking at its nutritional profile, you have to wonder if early humans were just lucky or if they had some fountain of knowledge that has been lost to time.

Cauliflower contains most of the vitamins and minerals the human body needs. It's high in fiber, antioxidants, and choline, which plays a huge role in brain development and producing neurotransmitters (which our nervous system needs). Cauliflower also has a low carbohydrate profile, which may also explain why it has become a popular substitute for grain and legume dishes.

- 2 medium-size cauliflower heads
- 10 tablespoons olive oil, divided
- 1 to 2 bulbs garlic, minced
- 1 tablespoon fresh or dried thyme
- 2 teaspoons ground cumin
- 2 tablespoons sea salt

Preheat the oven to 400°F (or use the convection oven setting).

Slice away the bottom of each cauliflower but keep the stem (do not core).

Set the cauliflower upright on its stem (like a tree on its trunk) and slice it lengthwise into ½-inch-thick slabs.

Pour 5 tablespoons of the olive oil onto each of two baking sheets and spread to coat evenly.

Spread the cauliflower steaks out on the baking sheets, leaving breathing room between each one. Flip each steak over (to coat with olive oil), and flip them over again.

Generously sprinkle the garlic over the top of each cauliflower steak.

Sprinkle each cauliflower steak with thyme, cumin, and sea salt.

Bake for 15 minutes, or until the steaks are golden brown, and then flip each steak and put them back in the oven for about 10 minutes. The cauliflower should be golden and crispy on the outside and gooey on the inside.

Let the steaks cool slightly. Serve immediately.

SAAG PANEER

Meaning "greens" in Sanskrit, saag originated in the Punjab region of northern India. It is said to have been a dish for farmers who needed a nourishing meal to strengthen their bodies and minds after laboring on long, hot days. The key ingredient in most saag dishes is garam masala, a special spice blend that differs based on region. In northern India it tends to be sweet and pungent, while in the south, hot red chilies make for a more fiery blend. You'll find that many garam masala ingredients, such as cinnamon, cardamom, and cloves, contain antioxidants and anti-inflammatory properties.[12, 13]

In Ayurvedic medicine, garam masala is believed to contain "warming" spices, which help increase metabolism and "digestive fire." Traditional Punjabi saag uses mustard greens, but any leafy green vegetable, including collard, dandelion, or Swiss chard, will work. Many traditional recipes also use vegetable oil or ghee, but we've chosen olive oil because of its array of health benefits. You can also add animal protein like chicken, lamb, or goat.

Saag is traditionally served with naan bread or over basmati rice.

8½ tablespoons olive oil, divided

1 teaspoon salt

1 tablespoon ground turmeric

1½ pounds baby spinach

16 ounces paneer cheese or firm tofu, cubed

1 medium yellow onion, chopped

5 garlic cloves, minced

2 tablespoons fresh minced ginger

⅛ teaspoon cayenne pepper (optional)

1½ tablespoons ground coriander

1½ teaspoons ground cumin

1 teaspoon ground cardamom

1 teaspoon garam masala

⅔ cup plain yogurt or plain oat milk yogurt

3 tablespoons honey

Sea salt and black pepper, to taste

3 cups cooked basmati rice

In a medium bowl, whisk together 4 tablespoons of the olive oil with the salt and turmeric. Add the paneer. Mix until thoroughly combined. Let the mixture sit at room temperature for about 20 minutes.

In a food processor or blender, purée the spinach with 1 to 2 tablespoons of water, scraping down the sides as needed, until it becomes a smooth paste. You may have to do this in batches.

In a Dutch oven over medium heat, heat 2½ tablespoons of olive oil. Add the paneer and cook for 5 to 7 minutes until golden, stirring occasionally. With a slotted spoon, remove the cheese and place it on a plate lined with paper towels.

Add 2 tablespoons of the olive oil to the Dutch oven. Add the onions, garlic, ginger, and cayenne pepper, if using, and sauté for about 10 to 15 minutes, until caramelized, stirring occasionally. If the mixture starts to dry out, add 1 to 2 tablespoons of water to keep it moist.

(CONTINUED)

NOTE: Paneer is a special, non-melting Indian cheese that you can find in most health food stores or those with larger cheese and dairy sections.

Add the coriander, cumin, cardamom, garam masala, and 1 to 2 tablespoons of water. Mix and then sauté for about 1 to 2 minutes, stirring occasionally.

Add the spinach purée and 1 cup of water. Mix well and cook for about 5 to 7 minutes, stirring occasionally.

Remove from the heat, add the yogurt, and mix well. Stir in the honey, and finally fold in the paneer.

Return the Dutch oven to the stove and heat the saag thoroughly over medium heat.

Season with salt and black pepper. Serve immediately over the basmati rice.

ESCAROLE LINGUINI

It looks a lot like lettuce, but escarole tastes quite different. As part of the chicory family, escarole is a type of endive that has a slightly bitter flavor. Historians believe escarole originated in either the Mediterranean region or in India. We know that Egyptians, Romans, and Greeks all grew this green, leafy vegetable, often using it in salads. Escarole contains several important nutrients, including copper, folate, and vitamins A, C, and K. It also supplies you with fiber, mostly insoluble.

Bitter vegetables, fruits, and herbs help improve the digestive process. The more bitter a food is, the more alkaline, and one of the common ways herbalists determine an ingredient's medicinal value is through its bitterness or alkaline level.

1 pound dried linguine

1 head escarole

6 tablespoons olive oil, divided

5 cloves garlic, minced

¼ cup parmesan, grated

Salt and pepper, to taste

Red chili flakes, to garnish (optional)

Prepare the pasta according to package directions. (If you're cooking with gluten-free pasta, strain in a colander and then run warm water over it to remove any extra starch.)

Meanwhile, prepare the escarole by removing the base and then washing the leaves in cold water. Spin, shake, or pat dry. Slice each leaf into long ribbons (one leaf should get you about 4 to 5 strips). You want to be able to twirl the strips with the pasta when eating.

Heat 2 tablespoons of the olive oil in a large skillet over medium heat and sauté the garlic for about 1 minute. Add the escarole to the pan. Use two big wooden spoons, toss the escarole as you would a salad to thoroughly combine it with the garlic olive oil. Then cover the skillet, lower the heat, and cook for about 7 minutes, or until the greens have cooked down (about half their original size).

Remove the cover and stir in 1 cup of water (a vegetable or chicken broth works great here too) and salt to taste. Then add the pasta and heat through for about 1 to 3 minutes.

(CONTINUED)

Remove from the heat and serve in bowls, topping each with 1 tablespoon of the olive oil and parmesan cheese. Serve immediately.

You may want to add some extra salt, and our family always adds crushed red pepper to taste.

NOTE: If you want to increase the protein, add 1 14.5-ounce can of drained cannellini beans when adding the pasta to the escarole.

MAJESTIC MUSHROOMS

*Nature alone is antique,
and the oldest art a mushroom.*

— THOMAS CARLYLE[1]

While walking through the woods, many of us have stumbled upon colorful and mysterious flora peeking out from the leaves or clustered at the base of old trees. For years, I would take quick note of these odd creations and go about my merry way. In the United States, at a young age, we're warned to stay away from mushrooms because many of them are poisonous. This is partly accurate—interspersed throughout the fungi kingdom are some truly toxic mushrooms that can make a person sick or even kill them. But this is why any mushroom hunter, veteran or novice, always carries a mushroom guide and double-checks with more experienced foragers before consuming newfound treasures. When in doubt, they always leave the mushroom in peace.

In the United States, it might be customary to fear or avoid local mushrooms, but travel to just about any other location and you'll find a different attitude—one that reveres mushrooms for their numerous medicinal and culinary powers. For instance, many European and Asian culinary centers embrace wild mushrooms as part of their gastronomy, and children are taught which ones to go after and which ones to avoid.

Man's fondness for toadstools is one of the oldest love stories on record. The earliest depictions of the relationship between humans and fungi may be a rock drawing found in the Sahara dating back 7,000 to 9,000 years, showing dancers holding mushroom-shaped objects. In ancient Egypt and Asia, mushrooms were made into a sacred tonic thought to prolong youthfulness.

(CONTINUED)

More than just a tasty food with an interesting texture, mushrooms are low in fat and calories and are highly nutritious, containing significant amounts of riboflavin, niacin, folate, iron, zinc, copper, magnesium, and vitamin B_6, to name a few.[2] Also high in fiber and potassium,[3] various mushroom extracts have been widely studied for their potential in the treatment of numerous ailments from migraines and mental disorders to cancer.

In 1991, the well-preserved remains of a 5,000-year-old man were found in the Ötztal Alps of Austria, and in his bag were two species of polypore mushroom, one with a string through the stalk.[4] He was given the nickname "Ötzi." This is interesting not only because it confirms prehistoric man's use of mushrooms but also because polypore mushrooms tend to grow on trees and are used mainly as medicine. In fact, researchers discovered that Ötzi suffered from intestinal parasites that would have likely caused stomach pain. Most tree mushrooms like the ones Ötzi carried are inedible because of their hardness; therefore Ötzi's possession of two different mushroom types points to a rather advanced understanding of the healing benefits of polypores.

The recipes in this chapter honor the sacred mushroom for its healing properties and delectable taste.

FOREST PORCINI AND FARRO

SERVES 4

According to an old Croatian mushroom hunting tradition, if you should ever stumble across a porcini in the forest, you must bend down and whisper, "Where is your brother?" because mushrooms always grow in pairs. Scattered throughout the forests of Europe, the porcini is a prized culinary fungus. Often found underneath a walnut tree, this fragrant mushroom is featured in dishes all over Italy and France.

As delicious as these mushrooms taste, they pack more than a culinary punch—they're high in antioxidants, including beta-carotene, ascorbic acid, and lycopene, that can help reduce chronic inflammation.

Studies also show that porcinis contain bioactive compounds that have been verified to possess antioxidant, antineoplastic (used to treat cancer), anti-inflammatory, antibacterial, and antiviral activities, plus these mushrooms protect the liver from damage.[5]

- 1½ cups farro
- 5 ounces fresh porcini mushrooms, or 3 ounces dried
- 5 tablespoons olive oil, divided
- 2 shallots, minced
- 3 tablespoons minced parsley, (plus a few extra tablespoons for garnish)
- 2½ cups chicken or vegetable stock
- ⅓ cup white wine
- Coarse sea salt and pepper, to taste

In a mixing bowl, thoroughly rinse and drain the farro grains to remove any unwanted debris.

To clean the porcinis, dampen a paper towel or thin cloth and rub the mushroom from the center of the cap outward toward the edges. For the stalk, move the cloth or paper towel downward from the top. If using dried mushrooms, simply add the mushrooms to a bowl and cover with boiling water to rehydrate. Let them sit for 30 minutes and then remove them from the water and pat dry.

Split the mushrooms into two separate portions. Roughly chop the first portion and gently slice the other.

Heat 3 tablespoons of the olive oil in a large skillet. Add the shallots and parsley. Cook until the shallots are soft and transparent.

Add the roughly chopped porcinis and sauté until lightly browned.

Add the farro and stir until it is fully coated with the olive oil. Add the stock and white wine, reduce to a simmer, and cover the skillet.

(CONTINUED)

Cook for 30 minutes or until the farro is soft. Add the parsley and season with salt and pepper.

In a small pan, heat 2 tablespoons of the olive oil on high heat. Add the sliced porcinis and sauté until soft.

Transfer the farro to four bowls and top with the mushrooms. Garnish with more fresh parsley, if desired.

SIMPLE CHANTERELLE MUSHROOMS

SERVES 4

One of the most sought-after mushrooms in Europe, Asia, and Australia, the chanterelle has been cherished for millennia. Its name originates from the Greek word *kantharos* or vase, most likely because of its shape. The chanterelle is not only enchantingly scrumptious but also possesses substantial medicinal value. Traditionally, chanterelles were used to prevent or treat cancer, reduce inflammation, kill microbes, stimulate or suppress the immune system, heal wounds, and treat respiratory tract infections.[6]

The flavor of this fancy fungi is so aromatic and delicious that the recipes built around it are usually simple, so as not to distract the tongue. This recipe falls right into that category. This is great as a side dish with any protein or as a savory sauce over pasta or rice.

3 tablespoons olive oil

2 tablespoons salted butter

1 onion, finely sliced

3 to 4 garlic cloves, finely chopped

1 pound chanterelles, cleaned thoroughly and chopped

2 ounces dry brandy

2 tablespoons finely chopped parsley

½ cup plain yogurt (or use the recipe on pg. 180)

Sea salt and black pepper, to taste

Heat the oil and butter in a medium frying pan over medium heat. Add the onion and garlic. Sauté until the onions are translucent, stirring constantly.

Add the chanterelles and cook for 5 minutes.

Add the brandy and parsley and simmer for 2 to 3 minutes.

Add the yogurt and simmer until thickened slightly, about 2 to 3 minutes. Taste and season with salt and pepper. Serve immediately.

NOTE: When hunting for chanterelles, many foragers believe that following smaller deer trails is the secret to success.

SAUTÉED MORELS WITH ELDERFLOWER AND MINER'S LETTUCE

SERVES 4

The morel mushroom grows in most of the temperate zones across America, Europe, and Asia. Almost brain-like in its squiggly texture, this tasty decomposer is the prized trophy of many a mushroom hunt and has become a time-tested spring tradition. Research has found that the morel mushroom sports some impressive healing properties, including boosting the immune system and fighting tumors, inflammation, and oxidative stress.[7]

SAFETY NOTE: Make sure to cook your morels fully before eating. They are somewhat toxic if eaten raw.

1 shallot, minced

¼ cup champagne vinegar or rice wine vinegar

½ cup olive oil, divided

2 teaspoons sea salt

⅓ cup elderflower syrup, agave, or honey

1 teaspoon minced fresh thyme

1 teaspoon cracked black pepper

1½ pounds miner's lettuce or endive

1 pound fresh morel mushrooms

In a small mixing bowl, mix the shallot and champagne vinegar and let the mixture stand at room temperature for 30 minutes to 1 hour. This will infuse the flavor of the shallot into the vinegar.

Add 5 tablespoons of the olive oil and the sea salt, elderflower syrup, thyme, and black pepper to the small mixing bowl. Vigorously whisk for 1 minute.

Clean the miner's lettuce and pat it gently to dry. Place in a large salad bowl.

Heat 3 tablespoons of the olive oil in a medium saucepan or skillet over medium heat. Add the mushrooms and sauté until lightly browned, about 4 minutes. If you are using dried mushrooms, first rehydrate them by placing them in a bowl of boiling water. Let them sit for 30 minutes and then drain off the water and pat dry before sautéing.

Add the mushrooms and the dressing to the lettuce and gently toss together.

GARLIC MUSHROOM DANDELION GREENS

The dandelion is native to Asia and Europe. The word *dandelion* comes from the French *dent de lion* or "lion's tooth," a reference to the plant's incisor-patterned leaves. Ancient physicians and herbalists were said to use dandelions to help treat liver and digestive ailments, toothaches, lethargy, and depression, and to stimulate the appetite. Recent studies show that dandelions have protective properties that may indeed help improve digestion while also fighting bacteria and viruses, reducing inflammation, and boosting the immune system.[8]

This dish pairs the powerful dandelion with the delectable shiitake mushroom, which hails from China and is believed to have first been cultivated between 1000 and 1100 A.D. Traditionally used in ancient Chinese and Japanese medicine, shiitakes were believed to strengthen the immune system, increase energy, extend life, and improve blood and circulation. Today, science is showing that shiitake mushrooms may in fact improve immunity,[9] and they may have properties that help prevent cancer.[10]

This recipe makes a wonderful side dish with meat like chicken or steak, or try mixing this with your favorite grain.

SAFETY NOTE: You can find dandelions year-round in most health food stores, but if you choose to wild-harvest your own dandelion greens and roots, make sure to pick from a safe location. Stay away from roadsides and unknown yards because toxic pesticides are often used to keep these "weeds" at bay.

4 tablespoons olive oil

5 cloves garlic, minced

1 red onion, chopped

3 ounces shiitake mushrooms, sliced

2 bunches dandelion greens, lightly chopped

½ cup red cooking wine

Sea salt and pepper, to taste

Heat the oil in a large skillet over medium heat. Add the garlic and onion and sauté until the onions are translucent and lightly brown, about 5 minutes.

Add the shiitake mushrooms and cook until softened, about 5 minutes.

Add the dandelion greens, red wine, and salt and pepper and stir. Cover the skillet and cook until the greens have softened, about 5 to 7 minutes.

Taste and season with additional salt and pepper.

THREE MUSHROOM STIR-FRY

SERVES 4 TO 6

We can thank the ancient Chinese for developing the art of stir-frying. Although it wasn't the most popular cooking technique in the East (that title went to boiling and steaming), stir-frying dishes is a healthy and delicious way to ensure you're feeding your body a balanced meal.

This recipe is loaded with ingredients that can help boost your immune system, like the maitake mushroom, also known as hen-of-the-wood. Maitake actually means "dancing mushroom" in Japanese, and as the legend goes, ancient foragers literally danced for joy upon finding this gem in the woods.

Today, Hui Shu Hua, as it's called in Chinese medicine, is lauded by health practitioners because it's rich in beta-glucans that may help activate and stimulate white blood cells, including macrophages, T-cells, natural killer cells, and neutrophils—all critical to keeping your immune system robust.[11]

Shiitake mushrooms also have a powerful effect on the immune system,[12] so this recipe gives you a one-two punch. Throw in some garlic and ginger—two herbs that also help bolster your defense system—and you're well on your way to warding off those pesky infections.

2 tablespoons oyster sauce

1 tablespoon soy sauce

½ teaspoon fish sauce

1 teaspoon toasted sesame oil

2 tablespoons minced garlic

2 tablespoons minced fresh ginger

8 ounces shiitake mushrooms, thinly sliced

8 ounces maitake mushrooms, thinly sliced

8 ounces oyster mushrooms, thinly sliced

1½ cups chopped bok choy

1 medium onion, sliced

½ cup carrots, shredded

1 cup broth of choice

2 tablespoons grapeseed oil

3 cups cooked brown rice

....

Whisk together the oyster sauce, soy sauce, and fish sauce in a small bowl.

Heat the sesame oil in a large skillet or wok over medium-high heat. Add the garlic and ginger and gently sauté for about 1 minute until golden and fragrant.

Add the mushrooms, bok choy, onion, and carrots to the skillet and sauté for 5 minutes, stirring occasionally. Add the broth. Cover and cook for 5 minutes.

Remove the cover and add the sauce mixture. Mix well and cook for 1 to 2 minutes. Then add the grapeseed oil and combine.

Season with salt and pepper to taste. Serve over brown rice.

DUXELLES

The magic of this dish is not only in its taste but also its versatility. Duxelles is perhaps best known in the classic English dish Beef Wellington, where the finely chopped mushroom and shallot concoction is spread on top of the beef before it's wrapped in pastry and baked.

This dish features portobello and cremini mushrooms, but you can opt for most any mushroom, including white button, lion's mane, chanterelle, or maitake. It also calls for vermouth, which is a digestive tonic first used by herbalists to help treat stomach issues and intestinal parasites. A fortified wine, vermouth has traditionally been flavored with some major healing herbs such as wormwood and skullcap. (Vermouth recipes often differ and may include other ingredients, so be sure to check the label on your bottle to learn what's hiding inside.)

Wormwood is believed to help fight pain[13] and inflammation,[14] while skullcap may help reduce anxiety[15] and fight bacteria and viruses.[16]

Believed to have been created by a French chef in the 1600s and named after the French general the chef worked for, duxelles can be used as a topping for meat (it pairs especially well with steak), as a dip or spread, mixed with scrambled eggs, or tucked inside an omelet.

4 portobellos, finely chopped

16 ounces cremini, finely chopped

3 tablespoons salted butter or ghee

6 large shallots, finely chopped

8 fresh thyme sprigs, stems removed

½ cup dry vermouth

Sea salt and black pepper, to taste

Place the mushrooms in the center of some cheesecloth and gather all the corners to create a bundle. Twist to wring out any moisture.

Melt the butter in a Dutch oven over medium-high heat. Add the mushrooms, shallots, and thyme. Sauté for about 10 minutes, until the moisture from the mushrooms has been mostly removed.

Add the dry vermouth and continue heating until the majority of the liquid has been reduced. Add salt and pepper to taste. Serve warm.

MUSHROOM TAPENADE

SERVES 8

This recipe features two superfoods: mushrooms and olives. Considered to be one of the oldest cultivated trees, dating back at least 7,000 years, olives originated in what we now know as Syria, Iran, and Palestine before spreading to the Mediterranean region and Africa. Olives (and olive oil) were an important staple in many ancient cultures, where you could find them served as part of a meal or featured in religious ceremonies and rites. Ancient Egyptians used olive oil for sacrifices and funerals, while the Bible and Koran both mention and praise the olive tree and its fruit. Olive oil was also prized for medicinal reasons. Ancient Greeks believed it could help treat cramps, wounds, and insomnia.

Thousands of years later, olive oil remains one of the healthiest foods we can incorporate into our diets, containing many antioxidants and possibly helping reduce the risk of chronic diseases,[17] strokes and heart disease,[18] and cancer.[19]

4 cups mushrooms of choice (we like oyster, chanterelle, and maitake)

5 cloves garlic, crushed

⅓ cup olive oil, divided

1 whole lemon, squeezed

½ cup chopped walnuts

½ cup kalamata olives (pitted)

1 teaspoon red wine vinegar

3 sprigs fresh thyme, stems removed

Sea salt and pepper, to taste

....

Preheat the oven to 450°F.

In a bowl, toss the mushrooms and garlic with half the olive oil (about 2 tablespoons plus 2 teaspoons).

Pour the mushrooms and garlic onto a cookie sheet and roast them in the oven for 10 to 12 minutes, until lightly browned.

Remove the mushrooms and garlic from the oven and let them cool. Once cooled, pour them into a food processor or blender.

Add the rest of the ingredients to the blender. Blend on low until the contents are fully processed. Season with salt and pepper to taste.

Serve with crusty bread or crackers.

SOUPS AND STEWS FOR THE SOUL

*In my grandmother's house
there was always chicken soup,
And talk of the old country—
mud and boards, Poverty,
The snow falling down the necks of lovers.*

— LOUIS SIMPSON

Making soup is probably almost as old as cooking itself. Anthropologists estimate soups date back *at least* 25,000 years. The only culinary practice that trumps a bubbling cauldron is directly roasting meat and vegetables over an open flame.

With the exception of some minor tweaks, tossing bones and meat scraps into a vat of water with herbs and roots has remained largely unchanged over the past 25 millennia. This cooking technique was ideal for stretching limited ingredients and for extracting vital nutrients from those ingredients (think bone broth), and as medicine. In Chinese medicine, for instance, it's believed that boiling herbs and roots with fresh vegetables, meat, and bones to create nourishing soups can aid in restoring vitality, fighting off infections and illnesses, soothing upset stomachs, and promoting overall health and wellness.

But broths, soups, and stews aren't just for our physical bodies. When you're feeling a bit blue or under the weather, saddling up to a steaming bowl of soup nourishes the soul.

FOLK HEALING SOUP

The origins of this recipe are hard to pin down. The ingredients have been featured in dishes throughout western Europe for the past 2,000 years. The blend of herbs and vegetables that this recipe calls for could have been found in the rugged pots of traveling caravans or elegant serving bowls of the ruling elite.

The spices in this soup tell a fascinating story, each with origins stretching across Europe and deep into Asia. Cinnamon, native to Sri Lanka, can lower blood pressure[1] and improve blood sugar levels, especially in type-2 diabetics.[2] Turmeric, from the tropical regions of Southeast Asia, can help with depression.[3] Saffron, believed to have originated in Iran, contains powerful antioxidants (including crocin and crocetin) that may protect brain cells and lower inflammation.[4]

The ancient spice routes, many of which are still being discovered today, are the unsung heroes that made flavorful and nutritious soups like this recipe possible for thousands of years.

NOTE: To give this soup a whole new character, try substituting all the spices with 2 to 2½ tablespoons of Berbere Spice (see page 192).

- 2 tablespoons olive oil
- 1 onion, chopped
- 5 cups low-sodium vegetable stock, divided
- 1 teaspoon ground cinnamon
- ½ teaspoon curry powder
- 1½ teaspoons ground turmeric
- ⅛ teaspoon cayenne pepper
- 1 tablespoon grated ginger
- 1 bay leaf
- 3 medium potatoes, diced
- 4 medium tomatoes, seeds removed and diced
- 2 celery stalks, sliced into half moons
- 2 carrots, sliced into thin rounds
- 1 14-ounce can chickpeas, drained and juice reserved
- 4 strands saffron
- 1 tablespoon lemon juice
- Salt and pepper, to taste
- Cooked barley or wild rice (optional)
- Fresh chopped herbs like parsley or cilantro (optional)

....

In a large pot, heat the olive oil over medium-high heat and add the onion. Sauté for 3 to 5 minutes until fragrant and slightly golden. Add 1½ cups of the vegetable stock and simmer for 20 minutes.

In a small bowl, combine the cinnamon, curry, turmeric, cayenne, ginger, and 2 tablespoons of the vegetable stock. Stir well. Add to the simmering stock and onions.

Pour the remaining vegetable stock into the pot, add the bay leaf, and bring to a boil. Reduce the heat to a simmer.

Add the potatoes, tomatoes, celery, and carrots. Simmer until the carrots are tender (about 20 minutes). Remove the bay leaf.

Add the chickpeas, saffron, and lemon juice and simmer for 10 minutes. Season with salt and pepper.

If using, add the barley to each bowl and then ladle the soup over the top. Garnish with fresh herbs.

SAVORY SEAWEED BROTH

SERVES 10

Contributed by Tara Lanich-LaBrie, herbalist, forager, and small farmer. Learn more about Tara's work at themedicinecircle.com.

When you want to improve digestion, boost the immune system, balance emotions, and feel more relaxed, consider reaching for broth. It's one of the simplest and purest ways to get concentrated herbal healing into your everyday diet. Whether you sip broth from a bottle at work or use it as a base for your favorite dishes, you're nourishing your mind and body with ingredients you might not regularly consume like seaweed, turmeric, nettle leaf, and calendula flowers. This medicinal broth features seaweed, which the Japanese have turned to as medicine and food for thousands of years. The ancient Japanese would make a paste out of seaweed and use it to treat burn wounds. This is understandable given that seaweed contains antibacterial properties. You'll also find iodine and the amino acid tyrosine, which together make two key hormones that help the thyroid function.

This is one of my favorite flavorful and nutrient-dense broths for helping build immunity and reduce inflammation, plus it serves as a rich base for many soups and stews. You can also drink this broth in the morning with a spoonful of miso or a sprinkle of salt. I make this mineral-rich broth once a week, especially during the winter months. Many of the dried herbs, flowers, and mushrooms can be purchased online in bulk.

1 large onion, halved

½ acorn, butternut, or other winter squash roasted in the oven, seeds removed, roasted, skin still on (about ½ cup)

1 celery stalk, chopped

3 cups dried seaweed (e.g., kombu, Alaria, or digitata kelp)

2 cups dried mushrooms or 4 cups fresh (e.g., shiitake, porcini, or lion's mane)

¼ cup calendula flowers

½ cup loose, dry nettle leaf or 2 cups fresh nettles

3 to 4 whole garlic cloves, peeled

1 tablespoon fresh minced ginger

4 sprigs fresh thyme or 1 teaspoon dried

1 to 2 sprigs fresh oregano (or wild oregano, monarda fistulosa) or ½ teaspoon dried

1 tablespoon dried sage

1 teaspoon or more salt, to taste

OPTIONAL

1 to 2 tablespoons fresh turmeric root or 1 tablespoon ground

1 whole fresh burdock root, chopped, or 1 to 2 tablespoons dry root

¼ cup fresh dandelion leaf or 2 tablespoons dry leaf

1 to 2 tablespoons ground dandelion root (not roasted)

1 to 2 tablespoons dried astragalus root powder

Combine all the ingredients along with 16 cups of water in a crock pot, set it on low, and cook for 2 to 3 hours or overnight. Or combine all the ingredients along with 16 cups of water in a large pot on the stovetop and simmer on low for 3 to 4 hours.

Strain and press as much goodness as possible through a mesh sieve.

(CONTINUED)

Salt to taste and add a squeeze of lemon or 1 tablespoon of miso (do not simmer or boil miso as the enzymes are alive).

Serve in a mug with 1 tablespoon miso (optional).

NOTE: If you're using a combination of mushrooms, check the flavor profile first. Some mushrooms like reishi have a more bitter flavor, so add a smaller amount if you are sensitive to that taste.

TRADITIONAL BERBER TAGINE

SERVES 4

Scattered across North Africa in Morocco, Algeria, Tunisia, Libya, Egypt, Mali, Niger, and Mauritania live the Berbers, indigenous people who have existed since before recorded history. It's believed the Berbers descended from people who lived in the region since the Neolithic age. Although the Berbers have dwelled in the mountains and desert for thousands of years, historians have no idea where they originated.

A roaming people, many Berbers call themselves *imazighen*, or "men of the land." Traditionally their cuisine was quite simple, based on corn, barley, sheep's milk, honey, goat cheese, and game meat. Tagines, named for the traditional clay pot used to make this dish, are slow-cooked stews made from spiced meat and vegetables. Although this dish came from the Berbers, it became a popular staple across northern Africa.

This filling recipe features chickpeas, one of the best plant-based protein sources (next to black beans and lentils) and filled with fiber, which is essential for a healthy digestive tract and happy gut. It also includes butternut squash, which is loaded with vitamin A, good for cell growth, vision, and supporting a healthy immune system.[5]

- 3 tablespoons olive oil
- 3 potatoes, peeled and sliced
- 3 carrots, sliced in ¼-inch rounds
- 2 medium onions, chopped
- 3 garlic cloves, minced
- 1 butternut squash, peeled, seeded, and cubed
- 1 15-ounce can garbanzo beans with juice
- 1 14.5-ounce can diced tomatoes with juice
- 1 cup vegetable broth
- 2 tablespoons fresh lemon juice
- ½ teaspoon salt
- 1 teaspoon ground coriander
- ½ teaspoon fresh turmeric, minced
- 1 teaspoon paprika
- ⅛ teaspoon cinnamon
- 1 teaspoon ground cumin
- ½ teaspoon minced fresh ginger
- Dash of cayenne pepper
- ¼ cup chopped cilantro

Add the olive oil to a large skillet over medium heat. Add the potatoes, carrots, onions, and garlic and sauté for about 15 minutes or until lightly browned.

Add the squash, garbanzo beans, and tomatoes with the vegetable broth and lemon juice to the skillet and mix. Add the salt, coriander, turmeric, paprika, cinnamon, cumin, ginger, and cayenne pepper.

Cover the mixture and bring it to a boil. Reduce to a simmer and cook for 30 minutes, or until the vegetables are tender.

Taste and season with salt and pepper. Garnish with chopped cilantro.

NOTE: This dish is typically served over couscous. If you're gluten free, try quinoa.

MEDICINAL YELLOW CURRY

Curry is famously associated with India, except there is no one recipe for this dish, and the word doesn't even exist in the Indian language. Curry is actually a catch-all, blanket term that came from British colonizers who used it to describe all stew-like dishes despite their vast differences. Today, curries generally refer to a spiced meat and/or vegetable dish that usually includes a sauce. Travel throughout India, Thailand, and Malaysia and you'll find different flavors and combinations. In northern India, many recipes call for water and blending tomatoes and onions to make a thick sauce, while in southern India, curries more often feature coconut milk. However, many curries share common ingredients, including chili paste, ginger, turmeric, and vegetables. This recipe is a hybrid that a chef friend shared with us, and we've added more herbs for extra flavor and health benefits. This recipe also features coconut oil, which has antioxidants that may help reduce inflammation and decrease the risk of developing chronic diseases, including heart disease.[6] Coconut oil may also possess antimicrobial and antibacterial properties.[7]

2 teaspoons coconut oil

½ teaspoon cumin seeds

2 cloves garlic, minced

2 tablespoons minced fresh ginger

1 red onion, chopped

2 teaspoons finely chopped fresh turmeric or 1½ tablespoons ground

1 teaspoon garam masala

1 teaspoon sea salt

2 red peppers, sliced

1 large eggplant, sliced into ½-inch cubes

3 medium carrots, sliced

2 tablespoons Thai green chili paste

2 14-ounce cans coconut milk

2 tablespoons honey

2 cups chopped spinach

Soy sauce or sea salt, to taste

½ cup fresh basil leaves

Cilantro to garnish

In a large skillet, add the coconut oil and cumin seeds. Cook on medium heat until the seeds are lightly toasted, about 10 minutes.

Add garlic and ginger. Sauté for 5 minutes, or until garlic is lightly browned. Add the red onion and sauté until translucent.

Add the fresh turmeric, garam masala, and salt. Cook for 5 minutes.

Add the peppers, eggplant, and carrots. Cook for 3 minutes.

Add the Thai green chili paste, coconut milk, honey, and enough water to barely cover the vegetables. Place a lid on the pan and simmer for 15 minutes, or until the veggies are tender.

Add the spinach and cook for 2 more minutes. For a thinner sauce, add water until you reach your desired consistency. Add soy sauce to taste.

Serve over basmati rice (or another nutritious grain). Top each bowl with fresh basil leaves and cilantro.

SAVORY WINTER LENTIL SOUP

SERVES 6

The lentil is one of the oldest food sources in human history. A majority of the ingredients we use today were cultivated after humans settled into agrarian societies and began planting and harvesting on a seasonal calendar. But there are some ingredients that were pivotal food staples of our ancestors long before they became farmers.

We're talking about primal foods that hunters and gatherers treasured for taste and nutrition. The everyday lentil, as plain as it might seem, is a member of that special group of ancient foods.

Evidence shows that hunter-gatherers in northern Africa and nearby regions of Asia consumed forms of wild lentils over 13,000 years ago. When we peek at the nutritional profile of this tiny but strong legume, we learn that it's one of the most protein-rich legumes in existence. In its dried form, it's 26 percent protein, making it a fantastic food for non-meat eaters. You'll also find iron, vitamin B$_6$, potassium, magnesium, calcium, phosphorus, lysine, and folate jammed into this tiny package. Plus, lentils are filled with dietary fiber, which the healthy bacteria living in your gut microbiome will thank you for.[8]

5 cups vegetable or chicken stock

2 celery stalks, diced

1 yellow onion, diced

1 butternut squash, diced

1 large bunch Swiss chard (1 to 1½ pounds), cut into small strips

1 14.5-ounce can diced tomatoes

3 cups French lentils

3 tablespoons curry powder

1 sprig fresh thyme

Salt and pepper, to taste

2 bay leaves

2 tablespoons raw sugar

4 tablespoons coconut oil or ghee

....

Add the stock to a large stock pot over medium heat along with 5 cups of water.

Rinse the lentils in a bowl of cold water. Strain using a colander.

As the water and stock are heating, add the celery, onions, squash, Swiss chard, diced tomatoes, and lentils and mix well.

Add the curry powder, thyme, salt and pepper, bay leaves, raw sugar, and coconut oil and bring the soup to a boil.

Lower the heat so the soup simmers, and cover the pot. Cook for 3 hours, stirring every 30 minutes.

Taste and adjust the seasoning. Serve warm.

NOTE: Try adding ½ teaspoon of coconut oil and a pinch of crushed red pepper to each bowl right after you pour the soup.

NOURISHING BONE BROTH

SERVES 4

Bone broth has been a part of most ancient culinary traditions throughout history. Although somewhat time consuming to make, it's well worth it when you consider its numerous health benefits. Glycine, a nonessential amino acid, is a neurotransmitter that may improve sleep, reduce sleepiness during the day, and improve cognitive functioning such as memory.[9] Glutamine, another amino acid found in gelatin, is anti-inflammatory and can help maintain the gut lining,[10] healing and preventing "leaky gut."[11] The high calcium and magnesium content[12] makes this time-honored sacred soup a powerful healer.

This broth is a great base for many of the soup recipes in this chapter.

4 quarts water

2 pounds raw beef or chicken bones (ideally with a good amount of meat still on them)

1 small onion, coarsely chopped

4 carrots, coarsely chopped

1 celery stalk, coarsely chopped

1 lemon, cut into slices, or 2 tablespoons apple cider vinegar

7 sprigs fresh thyme

4 large fresh garlic cloves

2 bay leaves

Sea salt and black pepper, to taste

In a large stock pot, combine all the ingredients.

Bring to a boil and then cover, leaving the lid slightly cracked to allow steam to escape. Reduce the heat to low and let the soup simmer for at least 4 to 6 hours, occasionally spooning off the foam from the top.

Strain and remove the bones.

Let the broth cool and then refrigerate it overnight.

Optional: skim off fat solids from the top the next day.

NOTE: The soup will appear gel-like the next day due to the gelatin found in bone broth. Don't worry. Once heated, the gelatin dissolves again, leaving you with a warm broth.

IRISH BROTCHAN ROY FOLTCHEP SOUP

Loosely translated from Gaelic to mean "broth fit for a king," this traditional Celtic soup may date back as far as the ancient druids. The leek, one of the centerpieces of this recipe, is referred to more than any other veggie in the poetry and lore of colorful Ireland. Near relatives to garlic and onions, leeks may promote heart health and reduce inflammation.[13]

2 cups vegetable or chicken stock

2 cups goat milk or milk of choice

2 tablespoons steel cut oatmeal

4 large leeks

2 tablespoons butter

6 scallions, finely sliced

½ teaspoon ground nutmeg or mace

Sea salt and white pepper, to taste

½ cup heavy cream (optional)

Small bunch chives, snipped, and/or parsley, chopped (optional)

. . . .

Add the stock and milk to a large pot or saucepan over medium heat. Stir in the oatmeal and simmer gently for 10 minutes.

Clean and chop the white portion of the leeks into 1-inch pieces, discarding the green parts. Place the leeks in a large bowl of chilled water and allow them to soak for several minutes. Pull the leeks out of the water, leaving any residual sand and dirt behind, and pat dry with a towel.

Melt the butter and gently sauté the leeks in a skillet over medium heat, until slightly soft (about 5 minutes). Add the scallions and nutmeg and sauté for 1 to 2 minutes, until softened.

Add the leeks and scallions to the oatmeal mixture. Stir to combine. Continue cooking for 20 minutes, stirring occasionally. Do not allow the contents to come to a boil.

Season with salt and white pepper. Stir in the cream, if using.

Ladle into bowls and garnish with chives and/or parsley, if using.

NOTE: If you're vegan, try substituting equal amounts of almond milk for the goat milk and vegan shortening for butter.

TRADITIONAL MĀORI PUHA BOILUP

SERVES 6 TO 8

Around 1250 A.D. it's believed that the Māori people traveled from Polynesia to New Zealand. Isolated from other humans, the Māori developed their unique culture over the following seven centuries, including language, mythology, customs, and art. In their early history, the Māori were quite dynamic. Not only did they hunt and gather food but they also maintained large community gardens filled with vegetables like sweet potato and taro root. There was no such thing as private property in Māori culture until European settlers arrived. Like many First Peoples, the Māori based their spiritual philosophy on a responsibility to protect the earth for the benefit of all life.

The Māori boil up is a traditional dish that has changed very little through the years. It's a soup that combines root vegetables such as kumara (or sweet potato) and leafy greens such as spinach or watercress with meat. Puha goes very well with a scoop of quinoa or wild rice mixed into each bowl.

1 whole chicken

2 tablespoons sea salt

1 bunch puha* (substitute with watercress)

1 bunch leeks, sliced into ½-inch pieces

1 kumara, peeled and diced (substitute with sweet potato)

½ onion, chopped

6 tomatoes, chopped

1 small pumpkin, seeded, peeled, and diced

3 scallions, thinly sliced

Puha is only available in Australia and New Zealand.

In a stock pot, add the chicken, salt, and 2 quarts of water and bring to a boil. Lower the heat and simmer for about 1 hour, or until the meat is falling off the bones.

Meanwhile, soak the puha (or watercress) in cold water for 5 minutes and then remove and dry it. Set it aside. Repeat this process with the leeks.

Remove the chicken from the pot and set it aside to cool.

Add the kumara, onion, tomatoes, pumpkin, and leeks to the stock pot and simmer for 15 minutes.

Separate the chicken meat from the bones and skin. Break the meat into large pieces and return it to the pot along with the scallions. Simmer for another 15 minutes.

Add the puha or watercress to the pot and stir to combine. Season with salt. Serve immediately.

AMERINDIAN PEPPERPOT

SERVES 6

This dish is legendary throughout the Caribbean islands and on the northern coasts of South America. Usually served on Christmas morning and other special holidays, pepperpot has its roots in the indigenous peoples and the slave trade, where people were brought from West Africa to the islands. While the ingredients may slightly differ depending on the country you visit, this recipe calls for cassareep, which is popular in Guyana.

Cassareep is a thick, dark syrup made from extracted liquid from cassava root. It was used not only in soups like the pepperpot but also in Caribbean folk medicine as an antiseptic.

Although it can be difficult to find, cassareep is well worth the extra effort and it's essential for achieving a delicious and authentic pepperpot. Try looking for it at gourmet markets or Caribbean specialty food stores, or purchase it online.

1 free-range chicken, deboned and chopped

½ cup cassareep (or substitute with molasses)

1 Scotch bonnet or habanero pepper

1 large onion, diced

2 sweet potatoes or yams, peeled and cubed

1 small bunch kale, cut into ribbons

1 small bunch fresh thyme, stems removed and chopped, or 2 teaspoons dried thyme leaves

4 garlic cloves, minced

½ teaspoon ground cloves

1 teaspoon ground cinnamon

2 dashes Angostura bitters

1 pound large or medium raw shrimp, peeled and deveined

Sea salt and black pepper, to taste

· ·

Place the chicken in a stock pot and add enough salted water to just cover the chicken. Bring to a boil.

Lower the heat and simmer for about 1 hour, or until the meat falls off the bones. Remove the chicken and allow it to cool. Separate the meat and discard the skin and bones.

Strain the remaining stock into another pot and add the cassareep, Scotch bonnet pepper, onion, sweet potatoes, kale, thyme, garlic, cloves, cinnamon, and bitters. Simmer for about 30 minutes.

Stir in the chicken.

Add the shrimp and simmer for 4 to 5 minutes, or until the shrimp are pink and firm to the touch.

Season with salt and pepper. Serve immediately.

NOTE: Traditionally a pepperpot is made from a medley of meats, including beef and pork. Ours uses chicken and shrimp, but feel free to use any meat combination.

TOM YUM SOUP

The Mediterranean diet often gets touted as one of the healthiest (for good reason!). But fly about 5,420 miles to the east, and you'll find another way of eating that is truly medicine for the body and soul. Traditional Thai cuisine features plenty of nourishing vegetables, lean animal and fish proteins, and herbs and spices known for their flavor and medicinal properties.

Tom Yum is not only one of the most popular Thai dishes worldwide, but it is also a true "super soup." Featuring coconut milk, which may have antimicrobial, anti-inflammatory, and antioxidant properties,[14] and immune-enhancing herbs, garlic, and cilantro,[15] it is an effective remedy for combating cold and flu viruses.

- 6 cups chicken or vegetable stock
- 1 stalk lemongrass, minced, using the lower ⅓ only (tough outer layer removed)
- 4 cloves garlic, minced
- 1 teaspoon red chili paste (or to taste)
- Juice from 1 lime
- 1 cup thinly sliced shiitake mushrooms
- 12 to 15 medium raw shrimp, shelled and deveined
- 1 green bell pepper, sliced
- 1 red bell pepper, sliced
- 1 cup halved cherry tomatoes
- 1 13.5-ounce can coconut milk
- 3 tablespoons fish sauce
- 1 tablespoon sea salt
- 1 teaspoon brown sugar or honey
- ½ cup roughly chopped cilantro

Pour the stock into a deep cooking pot and turn the heat to medium-high. Add the prepared lemongrass to the pot. Boil for 5 to 6 minutes, or until fragrant.

Reduce the heat to a simmer. Add the garlic, chili paste, lime juice, and mushrooms to the broth. Continue simmering for another 5 minutes.

Add the shrimp, both peppers, and cherry tomatoes. Simmer for 2 to 3 minutes, or until the shrimp are pink and plump.

Lower the heat and add the coconut milk, fish sauce, sea salt, and brown sugar. Simmer for 2 to 3 minutes. Taste and season to preference.

Serve in bowls with fresh cilantro sprinkled on top.

NOTE: You want to use jumbo shrimp for this recipe because of their immense flavor. Be careful not to overcook them.

TINY WONDERS
(LEGUMES, SEEDS, AND NUTS)

*The vegetable life does not content itself with
casting from the flower or the tree a single seed,
but it fills the air and earth with a prodigality
of seeds, that, if thousands perish, thousands
may plant themselves; that hundreds may
come up, that tens may live to maturity; that,
at least one may replace the parent.*

— RALPH WALDO EMERSON

Hold a bean, nut, or seed in the palm of your hand and you hold the entire life essence of that plant or tree—what it could one day become. When you eat these nutrient-dense foods, you're not just eating a bean, a nut, or a seed; you're taking in the entire potential life force that exists in that tiny, perfect package. Is it any wonder, then, that many ancient cultures found something powerful and profound in them?

Take the oak tree, for example. It was so important to the First Peoples of California and Oregon that it is known as "The Tree of Life." Most of us have been taught that acorns are poisonous, but they are actually edible when prepared in the right way. Many First Peoples will grind prepared acorns into flour to make a hearty and delicious bread.

Then there is the cacao tree, which the ancient Olmecs first cultivated, long before the Mayans and Aztecs did. The Olmecs, who lived along the Gulf of Mexico, used the cacao bean to produce a rich chocolate and spice elixir that was served during religious ceremonies and left in tombs. Cacao beans were so revered by the Olmecs that they would place the beans on the bodies of their dead, believing the bean would help "energize the soul and aid in the transition to the supernatural world."[1]

It wasn't just the peoples of the Americas who appreciated these potent kernels. Travel across continents and time and you'll find that legumes such as chickpeas and lentils were a staple in many Middle Eastern and Indian diets and religious customs. In the Jewish tradition, the lentil symbolizes the circle of life and is often eaten during mourning. In the Hindu faith, black sesame seeds are held sacred. Believed to absorb spiritual power and remove impurities, these tiny and tasty seeds are even mentioned in the ancient Vedas, and are thought to be the seed of immortality.

From mung bean to navy, red lentils to brown, walnuts to pumpkin seeds, beans, nuts, and seeds have played vital roles in feeding the bodies and souls of people throughout the ages.

INCA QUINOA SALAD

More than 6,000 years ago, the Incas of the Andes Mountains (historically one of the most powerful civilizations of the Americas) depended upon quinoa, this "mother grain," or *chisaya mama*, as their primary food source—the linchpin of their entire society and their connection to the gods. Quinoa had a multitude of uses for the Incas. Beyond its culinary status as a protein-packed plant food for hungry warriors, it was used in compresses for bruises, as a diuretic, and to treat liver and urinary tract problems, tuberculosis, appendicitis, and altitude and motion sickness.

Today quinoa continues to prove its worth as a top superfood thanks to its health-boosting properties. Although we often consider it an ancient grain, quinoa is actually a seed, offering an extremely nutritious balance of protein, heart-healthy fats, oil, and starch. It's also a great source of fiber, iron, phosphorus, B vitamins, potassium, calcium, vitamin E, and various beneficial antioxidants.

The benefits don't stop there. Amazingly, quinoa holds all nine essential amino acids in adequate proportions. Its high protein content (averaging about 16 percent, but reaching levels as high as 23 percent—more than twice the level found in common grain cereals) makes it one of the few vegetarian foodstuffs considered to be a complete protein, and pleasantly satiating at that.

- 1 cup quinoa, sprouted and thoroughly rinsed (Inca Red if you can find it)
- 1 cup vegetable or bone broth
- ¼ cup olive oil, divided
- ½ yellow or white onion, finely diced
- 1 small red bell pepper, finely diced
- 1 small green bell pepper, finely diced
- 1 tomato, diced
- 1 6-ounce can sliced black olives, drained
- ¼ cup chopped fresh cilantro and/or chives
- 1 jicama, peeled and chopped
- 3 cloves garlic, minced
- ¼ cup lemon juice (about 1 lemon)
- Salt and pepper, to taste
- ½ teaspoon ground coriander
- ½ teaspoon ground cumin
- 1 small jalapeño, finely chopped
- 1 cup chopped fresh Italian parsley
- 1 avocado, sliced into wedges

In a medium saucepan, combine the quinoa with the broth and 1 cup of water and bring to a boil. Reduce the heat and simmer covered for 10 minutes, until all of the broth is absorbed. Remove from the heat and let it sit covered for 5 more minutes. Fluff with a fork and set aside.

In a large saucepan, heat 2 tablespoons of the olive oil over medium heat. Add the onion, peppers, tomato, olives, cilantro, and jicama and sauté until soft, about 10 minutes. Add the garlic and cook for 2 minutes, stirring frequently.

Add the cooked quinoa to the vegetable mix. Cook over medium heat, stirring often, until just warmed through.

In a large serving bowl, combine the remaining olive oil, lemon juice, salt and pepper, coriander, and cumin. Add the quinoa mix and toss. Fold in the jalapeño and parsley, and season with additional salt and pepper to taste.

Serve warm or at room temperature, and garnish with avocado.

FERTILE CRESCENT FALAFEL

SERVES 6

Although the origins of falafel are hazy, it's believed to have emerged in Egypt, where it's made with fava beans. But travel across the Middle East and you're likely to find chickpeas or chickpea flour at the center of this beloved street food, snack, or breakfast.

Chickpeas have been used medicinally for thousands of years. In ancient Greece physicians prescribed chickpeas as diuretics, cleaning the kidneys and removing any sand or stones from them. In India chickpeas were used to treat indigestion, colds, bronchitis, and anemia. In China physicians also turned to chickpeas to aid the kidneys, remove kidney stones, and serve as a diuretic.

If you're searching for a food packed with protein, fiber, B vitamins, and manganese that will give you an energy boost while also sustaining you over the long haul, look no further than the chickpea. Modern researchers believe chickpeas may help control and reduce blood sugar,[2] reduce your risk of heart disease and diabetes,[3] promote brain health, and reduce anxiety and depression due to nutrients like magnesium,[4] selenium, and zinc.[5]

Serve these falafels with pita bread and topped with Tzatziki Sauce (page 208).

NOTE: It might be tempting to "cheat" and use canned chickpeas, but this will result in a mushy and less flavorful falafel that will disappoint your taste buds!

1½ cups dried chickpeas (don't use canned!)

½ onion, peeled and quartered

4 cloves garlic, crushed

2 teaspoons ground coriander

1 tablespoons ground cumin

½ cup chopped cilantro

¼ cup chopped parsley

2 tablespoons chopped fresh mint

1½ teaspoons salt

½ teaspoon baking soda

½ lemon, juiced and zested

Avocado oil for frying

Soak the chickpeas: Add the chickpeas to a large bowl and cover with water by 4 inches. Soak overnight. They will triple in volume once they finish soaking. For a shorter process called quick soaking, place the chickpeas in a pot and pour enough water over them to cover them by about 2 inches. Bring them to a boil and then remove them from the heat. Let them sit for 1 hour and they are ready to use.

Drain the chickpeas and transfer them to a food processor. Add all the remaining ingredients except the oil, and pulse until well combined. If the mixture needs a little moisture in order to pulse correctly in the food processor, add a few tablespoons of water. Be sure to keep the mixture as dry as possible, however. If there is too much water, the falafel will fall apart. You want the mixture to easily roll into balls.

Fill a large cast-iron or other skillet with 3 inches of oil. Heat over medium-high heat until the oil reaches 350°F.

Scoop out heaping tablespoons of the mixture and form into meatball-size balls (or form them into patties for "falafel burgers"). Fry in small batches until golden on each side.

Serve hot or at room temperature with pita bread and tzatziki sauce.

PINE NUT PILAF

When we think of pine nuts, we think about pesto—that delicious Italian mix of basil, pine nuts, olive oil, and parmesan cheese. But recent archaeological evidence has revealed that pine nuts and humans go back a long time. Archaeologists have discovered a sophisticated human enclave existing around 9000 B.C. in Utah. Inside Danger Cave, archaeologists uncovered well-preserved utensils, including leather straps, knives, milling tools, and archaeobiological remains that contained traces of pine nuts. Did you know that every pine tree produces an edible nut? Whether the nuts are from Macedonia, white bark, or Jeffrey pine, people across Europe, Asia, and North America have enjoyed the nutritional and medicinal properties of pine nuts for thousands of years. Some of the most famous ancient physicians, including Galen and Dioscorides, believed pine nuts could relieve chest pains and clear coughs and congestion.

Some say that the pineal gland in the brain got its name from the pine nut because they share an almost identical shape. According to the "doctrine of signatures," plant foods that resemble a particular part of the human anatomy tend to benefit that area. There might be some truth to this old wisdom. Research has found that pine nuts may help regulate blood sugar levels[6] and contain a healthy dose of omega-3 fatty acids, which are known to support better brain health.

- 6 tablespoons olive oil
- 2 medium red onions, finely chopped
- 4 large tomatoes (heirloom tomatoes are best), diced
- 4 cups vegetable broth
- 1 teaspoon fresh thyme leaves
- 2 cups red quinoa
- 1 cup pine nuts
- 2 bunches or 4 cups spinach
- Sea salt and pepper, to taste

Place a large skillet or saucepan over medium heat. Add the olive oil.

Add the onion and sauté until soft and transparent.

Add the tomatoes, broth, and thyme and bring to a boil.

Add the red quinoa, reduce the heat to a simmer, and cover the skillet. Cook for 1 hour or until all water has been absorbed or evaporated.

Place a separate, ungreased skillet over medium heat and add the pine nuts. Stir the nuts frequently, paying careful attention so they don't burn. It should take 3 to 5 minutes to toast the pine nuts. Once they're done, remove them from the heat.

Add the pine nuts and spinach to the large skillet and toss until fully mixed. Simmer for an additional 5 minutes, or until the spinach is fully cooked. Add salt and pepper to taste.

COMFORT KHICHDI WITH TOMATO ONION SALAD

SERVES: 2

Submitted by Mileen Patel, programming director, Sacred Science.

Travel throughout India and you're bound to come across many variations of this humble yet restorative dish. Combining basmati rice, lentils, vegetables, and spices and herbs, khichdi (also known as kitchari) is a staple meal in the ancient healing practice of Ayurveda. It's highly recommended for people recovering from illness or struggling with digestion.

In Ayurveda it's believed that this dish cleanses the physical body and helps rebalance the internal body. Khichdi is also eaten as a fasting food, and it is a "clean" meal when you're feeling under the weather or need to give your digestive system a break. It's even used to help people when they're in mourning because it's a versatile dish that's easy to make in large quantities and is deeply nourishing.

⅔ cup uncooked white basmati rice (long grain, preferably grown in India)

⅓ cup mung daal (split yellow lentils)

1 teaspoon ghee or salted butter

5 whole black peppercorns

5 whole cloves

1 to 2 garlic cloves, minced

2 to 3 small cinnamon sticks

2 teaspoons sea salt

½ teaspoon ground turmeric

....

Combine the rice and lentils in a saucepan or pot.

Rinse the mix in cool water until the water is clear. (This is one of the best rituals in the cooking process—getting your hands to repeatedly touch the food by covering the mix with water and then swirling it around for about 15 to 20 seconds. Then dump the water, and repeat the process 4 to 5 times.)

Once the runoff water is clear, drain the mix.

Add 3 cups of water and let the rice and daal soak for 20 to 30 minutes. The longer it soaks, the fluffier this mixture will be.

Place the pot on the stove and turn the burner on to high heat.

Add the ghee, peppercorns, cloves, garlic, cinnamon sticks, salt, and turmeric and stir to combine.

Bring the mixture to a boil and then turn the heat down to low and cover. Simmer until the water is boiled off (about 20 minutes). You may have to open the lid a couple of times to make sure it doesn't boil over. I generally poke in there once or twice toward the end with a fork to check the bottom to make sure there's no water left.

(CONTINUED)

Once the water has boiled off, turn off the stove and let the rice and daal sit, covered, for about 5 minutes.

Remove the lid and serve hot.

NOTE: To make a big batch of the rice and daal mix, go with 2 parts rice to 1 part daal, and then 3 parts water to 1 part of the mix.

TOMATO ONION SALAD

This recipe pairs well with the Comfort Khichdi.

- 1 medium white or yellow onion, chopped
- 1 medium Roma tomato, peeled, seeded, and chopped
- 1 teaspoon finely chopped cilantro
- 2 tablespoons lemon or lime juice
- ½ teaspoon roasted ground cumin
- ½ teaspoon ground coriander seed
- ¼ teaspoon finely ground salt, to taste

Combine the onion, tomato, and cilantro in a bowl.

Add the lemon juice, cumin, and coriander and stir.

Just before you're ready to eat, add the salt and mix. If you add the salt too early, the salad will become watery. Serve it as a side or put a few spoonfuls on top of each bowl of khichdi.

LEMON QUINOA SALAD
WITH HEMP SEED

SERVES 6

Quinoa was believed to be so important to the prosperity of the Incan Empire that the emperor would sow the first seeds of the season. The word *quinoa* comes from the Quechua word *kinwa*, and due to its nutrient density and other powerful health benefits, the United Nations (UN) has dubbed this seed a "super crop." Because it's a low-maintenance crop, the UN believes quinoa could increase food security and encourage greater diversity in agricultural systems.

Quinoa is also quite versatile. It can be eaten warm as a hot cereal, or cold. It can be brewed into beer or ground into flour for baked goods.

This recipe also features hemp seeds, which the Chinese have used for food and medicine for more than 3,000 years. Rich in essential fatty acids (omega-3s and omega-6s), hemp seeds are also a good source of protein, vitamin E, and minerals, including phosphorus, potassium, magnesium, calcium, iron, and zinc.

¼ cup olive oil

¼ cup lemon juice

¼ teaspoon minced lemon rind

¼ cup fresh basil leaves

2 teaspoons Dijon mustard

1 tablespoon honey

¼ teaspoon sea salt (plus a little extra)

¼ teaspoon coarsely ground black pepper

3 cups cooked quinoa, cooled

1 cup fresh green peas, lightly steamed

½ cup hulled hemp seeds

2 cups fresh spinach, shredded or finely chopped

....

To make the dressing, add the olive oil, lemon juice and rind, basil, mustard, honey, salt, and pepper to a blender and blend until smooth and creamy.

Combine the quinoa, peas, hemp seeds, and spinach in a medium bowl and add the contents of the blender to this mix. Toss together thoroughly.

This recipe can be served chilled or at room temperature.

NOTE: With a hearty and flavorful salad like this, we often toss in a bunch of extra greens, like arugula and spinach, before serving.

ARABIAN HUMMUS

SERVES 4

After the soybean, the chickpea is the most widely grown legume in the world. It's believed that the chickpea has been grown in the Middle East for more than 11,000 years. Hummus, a rich, creamy dip or spread made from chickpeas and tahini paste, was first recorded in ancient Egypt during the 13th century. However, many countries, including Greece, Lebanon, and Turkey, prominently feature this dish in their cuisines.

Adding to the numerous health properties that the chickpea contains, this recipe uses tahini, made from toasted ground sesame seeds, which also originated in the Middle East. Recent studies have shown that tahini (and sesame seed extract) may contain antibacterial properties due to certain antioxidants[7] and anti-inflammatory compounds.[8]

This recipe comes from Nick's mother, Peggy Polizzi, and was one of the most beloved dishes at her restaurant, Plain Jane's.

2 to 3 large garlic cloves

1 can (15.5 oz.) chickpeas, drained and liquid reserved

3 tablespoons fresh lemon juice

¼ teaspoon white pepper

¼ teaspoon sea salt

3 tablespoons sesame tahini

⅓ cup of reserved chickpea liquid (approximately, depending on desired consistency)

Extra virgin olive oil, for serving

Toasted pine nuts, for serving

....

In a food processor, purée the garlic cloves as much as possible. This will help them incorporate thoroughly.

Add all remaining ingredients and process until completely smooth. If the hummus seems a bit too thick, add more chickpea juice 1 tablespoon at a time until the mixture reaches the desired consistency.

Transfer the hummus to a bowl. Drizzle with extra virgin olive oil and sprinkle with toasted pine nuts.

Serve with warm pita bread for dipping.

BURIED TREASURES

The beet is the most intense of vegetables.
The radish, admittedly, is more feverish,
but the fire of the radish is a cold fire,
the fire of discontent not of passion.
Tomatoes are lusty enough, yet there runs
through tomatoes an undercurrent of frivolity.
Beets are deadly serious.

— TOM ROBBINS

When we think of our hunter-gatherer ancestors, the image that pops into our minds is often that of humans eating lots of fruits, nuts, seeds, and meat. But tubers like potatoes, yams, and yucca may have played a bigger role in our evolution than many realize. Recent archaeological findings have discovered that ancient humans living 100,000 years ago in Africa were eating tubers, roasted over an open flame.

It makes sense that our ancestors embraced root vegetables. Tubers like white potatoes, beets, yams, and yucca are "stick to your ribs" food, offering much-needed nutrition and numerous vital minerals and vitamins.

Because these subterranean foods were great for stocking winter food stores in northern climates, the symbolism and ritual surrounding roots and tubers often pertained to the foresight, strength, and fortitude needed to withstand the long, harsh winter months.

Many ancient healers also stocked their shelves with roots, using them in teas, juices, pastes, and powders to treat wide-ranging ailments. For instance, the Incas had a method for freeze-drying potatoes under a cloth at night when temperatures dropped. Then the potatoes were ground into powder, called chuñu, that was used to treat ulcers, warts, spasms, and syphilis.[1]

There is also something to be said for eating roots during times when we feel ungrounded and untethered. Consuming root vegetables has a way of helping us feel more spiritually centered and rooted in the here and now.

SUMMER BORSCHT

SERVES 6

In folklore the beet is a symbol of love, partially due to its often red color and heart-like shape. In Greek mythology, Aphrodite, the goddess of love, was said to have eaten beets to retain her beauty. And it was believed that if a man and a woman ate from the same beet, they were destined to fall in love.

Was this connection between beets and the heart just fun and games, or was there something more? Recent studies show there's truth behind these stories. Beets are high in nitrates, and beet juice may help decrease blood pressure and improve heart health.[2] They also contain folate (vitamin B_9), which can lower the risk of heart disease and stroke.

2 pounds beets (about 8 medium), peeled, halved, and thinly sliced

2 teaspoons sea salt, divided

Juice of 3 lemons

2 teaspoons lemon zest

4 garlic cloves (whole)

¾ cup plain low-fat yogurt (optional)

1 small cucumber, peeled, seeded, and diced

Minced fresh dill or chives for garnish

....

Combine the beets, 7 cups of water, and 1 teaspoon of the sea salt in a soup pot and bring to a simmer. Cook for 30 minutes.

Add the lemon juice, zest, remaining salt, and garlic cloves. Continue simmering uncovered for 20 minutes.

Remove from the heat and allow the borscht to cool. Cover and chill. Taste and adjust the seasoning.

Remove the garlic cloves.

Place 2 tablespoons of yogurt, if desired, into the center of 6 chilled soup bowls. Ladle in the soup. Garnish with diced cucumber and fresh herbs. This will keep for 2 to 3 days in the refrigerator.

NOTE: Beets are also extremely good for healthy prostate functioning, making these a terrific addition to the diets of men over the age of 30.

ROASTED WINTER ROOTS

SERVES 6

Not only are rutabagas, turnips, Jerusalem artichokes, beets, and carrots some of the oldest root vegetables on the planet but the art of roasting is one of the most primitive methods early humans used to cook their food. This recipe features a medley of root vegetables like turnips. Originating in central or eastern Asia, turnips are high in vitamin C, fiber, and potassium, and some studies suggest that eating this vegetable may help lower your risk of certain cancers.[3] This recipe also includes rutabagas, believed to come from Russia or Scandinavia. They are high in dietary fiber, which helps improve your gut microbiome, and potassium, which can help improve your heart health.

2 turnips

2 Jerusalem artichokes

2 rutabagas

2 carrots

2 parsnips

3 red or golden beets

2 sprigs fresh thyme

3 sprigs fresh rosemary

6 tablespoons ghee, melted

4 cloves garlic, minced

Sea salt and ground pepper, to taste

....

Preheat the oven to 350°F.

Roughly dice the root vegetables into chunks of varying sizes.

Separate the leaves of thyme and rosemary from the stems and place the leaves in a small bowl.

In a large mixing bowl, add the root vegetables, herbs, ghee, garlic, and salt and pepper and toss vigorously with two spoons until fully mixed.

Transfer the vegetables to a parchment-lined cookie sheet and spread them out evenly.

Bake for 35 minutes, or until veggies are browned around the edges.

NOTE: A little trick for roasting any type of veggie medley is to broil them on high for the final 5 minutes in the oven. This will help them crisp and caramelize, which adds more flavor.

Q'ERO POTATO SALAD

SERVES 6

Although the Andes mountain range extends from Venezuela to the southern tip of South America, the term *Andean people* generally refers to those indigenous tribes descended from the Incan Empire. Often living at altitudes of over 10,000 feet, and in the harshest of environments, Andeans have uniquely adapted to life high above the world.

One such tribe is the Q'ero of Ausungate. Ausungate is one of two sacred peaks in Peru. Living at nearly 12,000 feet above sea level, the Q'ero are traditionally simple farmers and herders. Quite isolated from the rest of the world, the Q'ero have no organized religion per se, living in balance with nature and respecting all living things. They worship Mother Nature (what they call Pachamama). The Q'ero speak an ancient form of the Quechan language and believe themselves to be the oldest and purest of Incan descendants.

The Q'ero live in modest dwellings of clay and stone and are known to be extraordinary weavers. Amazingly, their diet—primarily a variety of potato and alpaca meat—combined with their rugged lifestyle has kept them extraordinarily healthy with an almost nonexistent incidence of cancer.

1 tablespoon sacha inchi oil (or substitute with sesame oil)*

1 pound purple or assorted mixed color potatoes, unpeeled, diced into ½-inch pieces

1 onion, finely chopped

½ to 1 teaspoon chili powder

1 clove garlic, minced

1½ cups vegetable broth

¾ cup quinoa, rinsed and drained

¼ teaspoon sea salt

Dash ground pepper

¾ cup frozen corn, thawed (leftover corn sliced from the cob is also great)

You can find sacha inchi oil at health food stores or online.

....

In a large skillet, heat the oil and sauté the potatoes, onions, and chili powder until the onions are soft, about 8 minutes. Add the garlic and sauté for another 2 minutes.

Add the broth, mix well, and bring to a boil.

Stir in the quinoa, salt, and pepper and return the mixture to a boil.

Stir, cover, reduce the heat, and simmer for 15 minutes.

Turn off the heat, add the corn, and let the dish stand, covered, for 5 minutes. Remove the cover and mix gently to fluff.

Serve warm or refrigerate and serve cold.

NOTE: If you have access to hominy, or large-kernel corn, that is a great addition to this dish. The heartier corn bits really add an amazing texture.

A TYPICAL WELL-STOCKED ROOT CELLAR

Want to up your root cellar game? Then consider filling your kitchen with these essential ingredients:

- Beets
- Carrots
- Chinese cabbage
- Garlic
- Ginger
- Horseradish
- Leeks
- Onions
- Parsnips
- Potatoes
- Pumpkins
- Rutabagas
- Squash
- Sweet potatoes
- Turnips

EGYPTIAN LOTUS ROOT SALAD

SERVES 4

The lotus root has ancient ties to Traditional Chinese Medicine, Ayurveda, and Egyptian medicine and lore. In the land of the pharaohs, lotus was eaten at banquets as a sacred symbol of rebirth. This fragrant flower opens fully at dawn and completely closes by the afternoon. The legendary flower and root contain mildly narcotic alkaloids that are alcohol soluble and are commonly infused in wines and tinctures. Over the past few thousand years, the culinary use of lotus root has spread.

Native to Asia, Australia, and parts of the Middle East, the lotus root is filled with potassium, antioxidants, folate (B_9), and protein.

Seeds of 1 fresh pomegranate

1 lotus root,* thinly sliced lengthwise

1 small red onion, thinly sliced lengthwise

Olive oil, to taste

Sea salt, to taste

Look for lotus root at health food stores or Asian specialty foods markets.

Place the seeds in a ziplock or nut milk bag* and squeeze them until they burst and release their juices. Strain the juice into a large salad bowl and discard the seeds.

Add the lotus root and onion to the bowl of pomegranate juice and toss them to evenly coat.

Drizzle olive oil over the top to garnish and season with salt.

You can find a nut milk cloth bag online or at most health food stores.

NOTE: If you don't have access to fresh lotus root, you can often find frozen lotus root in health food and Asian specialty stores.

QUECHUA YUCCA SALAD

SERVES 6

It's difficult to know where to begin when singing the praises of the yucca plant. According to a groundbreaking study of ancient yucca chaws, or quids (the stringy remains of chewed yucca leaves), it appears that the yucca plant has been used for more than 3,000 years as food and sacred medicine by almost every indigenous American culture from the Great Plains of North America all the way to the southernmost tip of South America.

Every part of the yucca plant has significant value. The flowers contain a high level of phosphorus, calcium, and vitamin C. The leaves contain substances called saponins, which, when mixed with water, create a detergent-like foam traditionally used as a soap. The yucca leaves, being extremely fibrous, were pounded, shredded, and dried to make brushes, baskets, mats, and ropes. The leaves were also brewed into medicinal teas used for joint pain and inflammation, and used topically as a poultice for skin sores or to stop bleeding.

And then there is the tuberous root of the plant, which provides a carbohydrate-rich food source containing a healthy mix of vitamins and minerals as well as phytonutrients like resveratrol, the antioxidant famously found in red wine.

SAFETY NOTE: Be sure to peel the tough brown exterior and first white layer and then fully cook your yucca, as it can be poisonous if eaten raw.

2 pounds yucca root, peeled and sliced lengthwise

½ teaspoon salt

¼ cup olive oil

½ onion, diced

4 cloves garlic, minced

1 sweet red pepper, chopped

½ teaspoon fresh lime juice

¼ cup finely chopped cilantro

In a large saucepan, add the yucca and fill with enough water to cover. Stir in the salt and bring to a boil over medium-high heat. Cover and cook until tender, about 15 minutes. Drain. Place the slices on a serving plate.

Meanwhile, in a medium skillet, heat the olive oil and add the onion, garlic, and red pepper. Sauté for about 5 minutes on medium heat until softened.

Add the lime juice and cilantro to the skillet and combine.

Pour the mixture over the yucca slices and serve.

NOTE: Make sure not to overcook your yucca. You want it to be firm but easy to mash; otherwise the salad will get mushy.

OVEN-ROASTED HERB FRENCH FRIES

SERVES 6

It's believed that at the height of its power, the Incan Empire stretched along the entire west coast of South America, from Colombia to the southern tip of Chile. And it's in the region we know today as southern Peru and northern Bolivia that the Incas are credited with cultivating the potato some 7,000 years ago. The Incas domesticated not just one, two, or three varieties but more than 3,000 distinct kinds that were grown, eaten, preserved (for up to 10 years!), and used medicinally. In ancient Incan medicine, fermented potatoes were used to treat infections and pneumonia and to help women heal after childbirth.

Potatoes have gotten a bad rap in recent years—through no fault of their own. Potatoes are one of the few vegetables that contain just about every nutrient (except for vitamin D, vitamin A, and calcium). They are high in fiber and are filled with antioxidants. Potatoes have been viewed as unhealthy because of how modern humans have cooked them.

But by oven roasting the potatoes with minimal oil and combining them with beneficial herbs, this recipe returns the humble spud to its healthier roots.

3 pounds potatoes, with skin, sliced into fries (your choice; we like to use red potatoes)

5 cloves garlic, minced, or 1 tablespoon dried

5 sprigs fresh rosemary or 1 tablespoon dried

3 sprigs fresh oregano or 1 teaspoon dried

4 tablespoons olive oil

Salt and black pepper, to taste

....

Preheat the oven to 450°F.

In a large mixing bowl, combine the sliced potatoes, garlic, herbs, and olive oil and toss well.

Place the potatoes on 2 parchment-lined baking sheets. Make sure the potatoes don't touch each other.

Place the baking sheets in the oven and roast the potatoes for about 13 to 15 minutes.

Remove the sheets from the oven, and push the tip of a spatula across the pan to loosen the fries from the pan and get some movement. Place them back in the oven for another 25 minutes.

Remove the potatoes from the oven and season with salt and pepper to taste.

NOTE: For crispier fries, make them smaller and reduce the cooking time.

GODLY GRAINS

From a tiny seed to dispersed pollen grains hoping to bloom someday—everything holds a story within it. We just need to observe a little more.

— SIJDAH HUSSAIN

The pursuit of food is considered to be the most fundamental initiator of human evolution. Like all other creatures, we need proximity to good hunting grounds, fertile vegetation, and reliable water sources. It's an innate survival tactic that's embedded within us—and for good reason. If you think you're facing uncertainty in your life today, imagine having to travel hundreds of miles because your sole source of sustenance, a pack of elk or a school of trout from a fishing hole, suddenly vanished.

Nowadays we take easy access to food for granted, but can you imagine what a relief it was when early agricultural methods came about? The concept of working with the seasons and soil to bring food out of the ground, year after year, must have been an almost miraculous notion 10,000 years ago. Instead of being consumed with the constant distraction of where the next meal would come from, our ancestors began to see some stability in their lives. A stability that would ultimately free up the brainpower and muscle needed for the next evolutionary leaps to be taken.

Although we associate grains with agriculture, humans ate wheat and rice long before the advent of farming. In North Africa and on the Mediterranean coastline of the Middle East, early humans gathered a variety of wild-growing cereals as part of their Paleolithic diet. The most common of these cereal grains was a species of wild barley, now thought of as the world's first cultivated grain.

The earliest evidence we have of the systematic cultivation and storage of barley was found in an 11,000-year-old town known as Dhra on the Jordanian banks of the Dead Sea. Remnants of old cisterns and silos containing both cultivated *and* wild barley have been excavated. It seems quite evident that this practice marked the beginning of "settlements," and from this fundamental shift in lifestyle, towns, cities, and great civilizations eventually sprung.

SASQU (DATE PORRIDGE)

Easily preserved, super sweet, and loaded with iron, the date was a popular fruit crop in ancient Mesopotamian life. The date was unique; it could survive in the extremely saline soils of this region. Stone tablets found at the ancient Sumerian palace of Mari (in present day Syria), depict one of the oldest breakfast foods ever discovered. Sasqu is a porridge made from either an ancient grain called emmer or barley; it was traditionally mixed with milk or oil to make it creamy. Dates and nuts were then added as a topping to give this yummy dish more sweetness and texture. It also boosted the nutritional profile of the dish. Dates are high in antioxidants and fiber, and may promote brain health.[1]

1¼ cups barley flour

4 cups milk or water (almond milk is a great vegan substitute)

½ teaspoon ground cinnamon

1 teaspoon vanilla

Sea salt, to taste

4 tablespoons wild honey

⅔ cup chopped dates

⅔ cup chopped walnuts

In a medium saucepan on medium heat, gently whisk together the barley flour and milk and bring them to a boil. Immediately reduce the heat to low and simmer for 5 minutes, stirring occasionally.

Remove from the heat and add the cinnamon, vanilla, and salt to taste. Top each bowl with wild honey, dates, and walnuts. Serve immediately.

NOTE: This is a great recipe for young children. You can also substitute maple syrup for the honey.

JUNGLE OATMEAL

SERVES 2

Submitted by Mileen Patel, programming director, Sacred Science.

Travel back 32,000 years and you'll find that our hunter-gatherer ancestors ate goats and bison, acorns, plums, and . . . oats? It's true. A team of researchers from the University of Florence in Italy discovered an ancient stone grinding tool in southern Italy that contained the remnants of ground-up wild oats. It's believed that the ancient Greeks used oats for the porridge we know as oatmeal.

Throughout the ages, various folk medicines have used oats to help treat depression and relieve nerve pain. Various cultures from ancient Rome to Persia would add oats to baths and creams, believing it could improve skin conditions. Traditional Chinese Medicine uses oats to help balance hormones and stabilize moods.

Today oatmeal has become a popular breakfast choice in the Western world. Oats have more protein than most grains and contain many antioxidants, including avenanthramides, which are almost exclusively found in oats. Research shows it may help improve blood pressure by widening blood vessels.[2] Oats also provide beta-glucan fiber, which may reduce cholesterol and blood sugar levels,[3] increase good gut bacteria,[4] and help you feel full.[5]

½ cup rolled oats

5 to 10 walnut halves, crushed

5 to 10 almonds, crushed

5 to 10 cashews, crushed

1 tablespoon butter or 1 teaspoon ghee

4 pinches ground cinnamon

2 pinches ground cardamom

1 to 2 pinches finely ground salt, to taste

1 banana, diced

⅛ to ¼ cup dried, unsweetened coconut flakes

1 to 2 teaspoons ground flaxseed

....

In a medium saucepan, heat 2¼ cups of water on high heat until bubbles start to form. Add the oats and nuts and turn the heat down to medium.

Simmer, stirring occasionally, for about 3 to 4 minutes, or until almost all the water has evaporated.

Turn down the heat down to low and add the butter, cinnamon, cardamom, and salt.

Stir until the water has evaporated, about 1 minute.

Add the banana and stir for about 30 seconds.

Turn off the heat and add the coconut flakes; stir for a few seconds to combine.

Add the flax and stir to combine. Serve immediately.

KAMUT BERRY SALAD

Kamut is an ancient grain most closely related to wheat. Its name comes from the Egyptian word *khorasan*, meaning wheat. Legend has it that grains of khorasan were found entombed in Egyptian pyramids and later grown by modern farmers. Egyptian farmers today will tell you that they have grown kamut for many generations. More digestible than wheat and with fewer calories, kamut is rich in protein, fiber, and minerals.

2 cups kamut berries or wheat berries

1 tablespoon salt, plus more to taste

1 butternut squash (about 2 pounds), peeled, seeded, and cut into ¾-inch cubes

6 tablespoons olive oil, divided

Salt, to taste

Black pepper, to taste

1 small onion, chopped

4 shallots, minced

2 teaspoons mustard seeds

1½ teaspoons curry powder

1½ teaspoons ground cumin

1 large tart apple, peeled and diced

4 tablespoons red wine vinegar

¼ cup white raisins

1 cup minced fresh parsley leaves

....

Rinse the kamut under cold running water for several minutes and then place in a medium saucepan. Add 6 cups of water and 1 tablespoon of salt. Cook and bring to a boil over medium heat. Reduce the heat and simmer until tender, approximately 2 hours.

Preheat the oven to 400°F. Lightly coat the squash with 2 tablespoons of olive oil and place it on a baking sheet. Season with salt and pepper to taste and bake for 30 minutes.

Coat a large sauté pan with 4 tablespoons of olive oil and heat on medium. Add the onion and shallots, season with salt and pepper to taste, and sauté until just soft. Add the mustard seeds, curry powder, cumin, and apple, stirring well, and continue cooking for about 1 minute or until fragrant.

Add the vinegar and stir to deglaze the pan and loosen the crispy bits from the bottom. Remove from the heat. Add the cooked kamut berries and stir well.

(CONTINUED)

Transfer the kamut berries to a large bowl. Add the butternut squash and raisins and toss to combine. Just before serving, top with the minced parsley leaves. This dish may be served hot or at room temperature.

NOTE: Try adding a scoop of our homemade yogurt from our recipe (on page 180) on top of each bowl.

PLANT-INFUSED POLENTA WITH MUSHROOM MEDLEY

SERVES 3

What is it about "peasant food" that continues to capture our taste buds and tickle our hearts? Perhaps these dishes unlock a long-forgotten connection to our ancestors, who had few possessions and lived difficult lives. Despite their hardships, long-ago humans found nourishment for their bodies and spirits in simple ingredients they transformed into magical meals.

Polenta falls into this category. It's one of the oldest dishes in recorded history. The ancient Sumerians made polenta first with millet and rye, but the dish we know today is said to have originated in Italy in the 1500s and is made from ground cornmeal. Polenta is cheap to make and very filling. It's rich in antioxidants,[6] it won't raise your blood sugar after eating,[7] and it's high in complex carbs,[8] which take longer for your body to digest so you feel satiated longer and have more energy.

- 1 cup polenta (or 1 log premade polenta)
- 4 tablespoons ghee, divided
- ½ cup freshly grated Romano or parmesan cheese
- Sea salt and pepper, to taste
- 3 tablespoons olive oil, divided
- 2 leeks, washed to remove grit and sliced into thin circles

- 16 ounces assorted mushrooms (a mixture of your favorites like chanterelles, porcini, oysters), sliced
- 1 cup chicken or vegetable stock
- Salt and pepper, to taste
- 2 garlic cloves, minced
- 2 bunches spinach, Swiss chard, or escarole (about 1½ to 2 pounds), finely chopped

To make the polenta, bring 4 cups of water and salt to boil in a large saucepan. Slowly pour the polenta into the water, whisking to combine. Reduce the heat to low and continue whisking until the polenta begins to thicken, about 5 minutes. Cover and cook for about 30 minutes, or until the polenta has completely thickened. Whisk occasionally until the polenta becomes too thick to whisk and then switch to a wooden spoon. Once it's cooked, remove the polenta from the heat and add 2 tablespoons of the ghee and the cheese, and season with salt and pepper to taste.

To make the medley, heat 2 tablespoons of the ghee and 2 tablespoons of the olive oil in a large skillet on medium heat. Add the leeks and sauté until softened, about 7 minutes. Add the mushrooms and sauté for another 7 minutes, until lightly browned. Then add the stock, season with salt and pepper to taste, and let simmer for an additional 10 minutes.

(CONTINUED)

To make the greens, heat 1 tablespoon of olive oil in a medium saucepan over medium heat. Add the garlic and sauté for 1 minute and then add the spinach. Cover and cook for about 5 minutes, until the spinach has softened. Remove from the heat and season with salt and pepper.

To serve, place the polenta in the middle of the plate, add the mushroom medley on top, and place the sautéed greens on the side.

ASPARAGUS RISOTTO

SERVES 4

Native to Africa, Europe, and Asia, asparagus and its 300 varieties have a long history in folk medicine. In Botswana and South Africa, for instance, asparagus was used to treat sores, infections, and tuberculosis. In India asparagus root was believed to promote fertility, relieve menstrual cramping, and act as a diuretic, helping flush the kidneys. When we look at the nutritional profile of asparagus, it's easy to see why our ancestors used it the way they did. Asparagus is 94 percent water, which helps hydrate the body. It's also rich in the vitamin folate (B_9), which helps create red blood cells and produce DNA. Folate is especially important for women early in pregnancy to help the fetus develop properly. Studies also suggest that asparagus may improve blood pressure, due to a compound that helps open blood vessels.[9]

This recipe pairs asparagus with arborio rice, named after the Italian town where it's thought this short-grain white rice originated. It's believed that rice made its way to Italy (and other European countries) by way of India. Arborio rice, though, is native to northern Italy, and is typically used to make the warm, creamy dish known as risotto—traditionally considered a peasant food.

This dish is hearty enough to eat as the main dish.

2 tablespoons olive oil

1 bunch asparagus, sliced into ½-inch rounds

5 cloves garlic, minced

4 shallots, thinly sliced

2 cups uncooked arborio rice

5 cups chicken or vegetable stock

1 tablespoon ghee

½ cup grated Parmesan or Romano or any hard Italian cheese

Salt and pepper, to taste

2 teaspoons lemon zest

....

Heat the olive oil in a large skillet over medium heat. Sauté the asparagus for about 15 minutes and then transfer to a plate. Set aside.

Add the garlic and shallots to the same pan and sauté until lightly brown, about 2 minutes.

Add the rice and cook for 1 to 2 minutes until the rice is slightly toasted. Add the stock one ladle at a time (about ½ cup per ladle), stirring after each addition until the liquid is absorbed. Repeat this process until there is one ladle of stock left. This should take about 18 to 20 minutes.

Remove from the heat and add the ghee, cheese, and salt and pepper to taste. Add the asparagus back in along with the lemon zest. Serve immediately.

CHOCTAW CORNBREAD

The story of cornbread can be traced to the First Peoples of North America. Corn is considered a sacred staple to most native people. Among the Choctaw tribe, corn is known as one of the "Three Sisters" because it's planted together with squash and beans. One Choctaw legend tells of the Ohoyo Osh Chisba, or the unknown woman, who gifted corn to the Choctaw people. In the story, two hungry hunters were sitting by a riverbed, contemplating their scanty, unappetizing meal. A luminous woman appeared bearing flowers symbolizing all their loved ones who had passed. The hunters approached her with reverence and offered her their food. She gratefully accepted a portion, and as thanks, told them to return at the next midsummer moon to the mound where she was standing. On their return, an unfamiliar plant had sprouted. This plant was corn, and it was prized and revered by the Choctaw people and eaten with gratitude from that day onward.

1¼ cups all-purpose white or whole wheat flour

1 cup yellow cornmeal

⅓ cup raw granulated sugar

½ teaspoon salt

1 tablespoon baking powder

1¼ cups milk, or unsweetened almond milk for a plant-based alternative

⅓ cup canola oil or applesauce

Preheat the oven to 400°F and lightly grease an 8 × 8-inch pan.

In a large bowl, stir together the flour, cornmeal, sugar, salt, and baking powder.

Slowly pour in the milk and canola oil. Mix gently until well combined.

Pour the batter into the prepared pan.

Bake for 20 to 25 minutes, or until a toothpick or skewer inserted into the center comes out clean. Let the bread cool and then serve.

NOTE: If you'd like to add a little extra pizzazz to your cornbread, stir in your favorite spice while combining the dry ingredients, or mix in some chunky corn kernels to the wet batter before pouring it into the pan.

SOURDOUGH BREAD

Contributed by Callie Longenecker, a chef, clinical nutritionist, and clinical herbalist. Learn more at earthenhands.com.

262 grams sourdough starter*

770 grams or about 3 ¼ cups of filtered water, (plus an additional 54 grams or about ¼ cup)

510 grams bread flour

500 grams whole wheat flour

25 grams sea salt

*See page 125 for how to make your own starter.

The relationship between humans and grains has changed quite dramatically over the past few centuries for many reasons. One is the promotion of more fast food and less fermented food. Along with hybridization and conventional farming practices, grains have, unfortunately, become more problematic. But grains have always played a part in ancient diets. While the men were hunting for meat, the women were in the field gathering grains and harvesting what they called "the staff of life." It was a labor of love—harvesting, threshing, winnowing, and pouring countless hours of attention into these plants. It was a staple for most people, as they prepared breads and porridges in a way that would most effectively nourish their families.

This always involved fermentation. Fermenting grains is the oldest style of preparing them. It breaks down their hard-to-digest components while maximizing nutrient bioavailability. Fermented grains are full of beneficial bacteria, which help nourish the gut microbiome and increase microflora diversity.

Sourdough bread is the oldest leavened bread. We can trace it back to at least ancient Egypt. Natural bacteria cause the dough to rise, making it easier to digest than other breads. Sourdough also contains more vitamins (especially B vitamins), minerals, antioxidants, fiber, and protein than other choices.

In a large bowl, combine the sourdough starter with the water. Cover and let it sit in a warm place (ideally around 74 to 76°F) for 35 minutes.

Add the bread flour and whole wheat flour. Mix until well combined, about 3 to 4 minutes.

Cover and let the dough rest for 35 minutes.

Add the sea salt and the rest of the water.

Knead until the salt and water are incorporated, about 3 minutes.

Cover and let the dough rest for 35 minutes.

Stretch the dough and fold it over onto itself. Cover and let it rest for 15 minutes. Repeat this twice more.

Place the bowl of dough in the refrigerator to rest overnight (at least 8 hours).

The next morning, transfer the dough onto a clean work surface and cut the dough in half. These are your two loaves. If you find that the dough is too sticky, you can dust it with extra flour. Roll each piece into a ball and push it across the surface, and then pull it back to you, creating tension with the dough. Repeat this step twice more. When you touch the dough with your finger, it should "bounce back."

(CONTINUED)

Let the loaves rest on the counter for 20 minutes and then shape them again, with the same method of rolling, pushing, and pulling.

Transfer the loaves to two banneton proofing baskets, dusted with flour. Cover them and place them in the refrigerator for 2 hours.

Preheat the oven to 450°F and place a Dutch oven in the oven to start heating.

Transfer one loaf of dough onto parchment paper and use a bread lame or a sharp paring knife to score a line down the center of the bread. You can also create beautiful designs on your loaf with the scores.

Lift the parchment-lined dough into the Dutch oven, cover, and bake for 22 minutes. Remove the lid and continue baking for another 10 to 14 minutes, or until the bread is golden.

Let the bread cool before slicing it.

MAKING A SOURDOUGH STARTER

To create a sourdough starter, you'll need flour, water, and time. It takes about a week to prepare a starter that's active enough to bake bread.

DAY 1: In a glass jar, mix 1 cup of flour with 1 cup of filtered water. Stir and cover with a cheesecloth or tea towel and let the mixture rest for 24 hours.

DAY 2: Discard half the mixture and repeat the same process, adding 1 cup of flour with 1 cup of water. Stir and cover.

DAY 3: Repeat Day 2

DAY 4: Repeat Day 2

DAY 5: Repeat Day 2

DAY 6: Repeat Day 2, but feed it every 12 hours instead of every 24. (You'll now empty half and then feed the starter with 1 cup flour plus 1 cup water, twice a day.)

DAY 7: Repeat Day 6 and start baking bread! You'll know it's ready when it's full of bubbles and doubled in size.

ESSENE SPROUTED WHEAT MANNA BREAD

SERVES 6

Talk about the epitome of ancient healing foods. When the famous Dead Sea Scrolls were recovered, there were a few passages that included an Essene recipe for a sacred "living" bread called manna. The Essenes were a mystic Jewish sect, and the recipe below is an adaptation of the original.

What separates this recipe from other unleavened breads is that the final product is never fully cooked, so it contains extraordinary nutritional value, including more minerals, vitamins, and amino acids than other breads. Kamut provides you with fiber and protein, while spelt also gives your body protein and essential nutrients, including iron, magnesium, fiber, and zinc.

One of the key elements to manna bread is sprouting the grains, which many people believe activates the life energy that each seed possesses. It's said that unsprouted seeds are in a dormant state and are not as digestible as they are once they've started to sprout. It's pretty astounding that this delicious and nutritious recipe came from a fragile 2,000-year-old scroll that was lying in a remote Middle Eastern cave.

The desired texture is for a crunchy outer crust and a soft and chewy inside. But everyone likes their manna a little different, so experiment until you hit perfection.

1 cup kamut berries*

1 cup spelt berries

Spring water

4 tablespoons olive oil

6 dried figs, chopped

½ cup soaked walnuts, chopped

1 tablespoon Himalayan sea salt

1 cup spelt flour

Look for kamut in health food stores.

....

The original Dead Sea Scrolls recipe calls for the bread to be "baked in the sun," but you can simulate this in your oven by baking the bread on a very low heat (I recommend 200°F) for 3 to 4 hours. During the last hour, turn up the heat up to 300°F to create a nice golden top on the bread.

Add the kamut and spelt to a medium bowl and cover with water until they're fully submerged. Leave the bowl on your countertop overnight to sprout the grains. (You will know the grains are ready when the small sprouts from each grain are ¼ inch long.) Drain off any excess water that has not been absorbed.

Place the olive oil, figs, walnuts, and sea salt in a large food processor and mix on high for 30 seconds.

Add the sprouted kamut and spelt to the food processor and continue mixing on high. Add a small amount of warm spring water if the ingredients stick together. Within a minute of blending, the contents should begin to resemble a dough. Transfer the mixture to a bowl and add the spelt flour. If it's too sticky, add a little bit more flour; if it's too dry, add a few tablespoons of water.

(CONTINUED)

Remove the dough from the food processor, separate it into even-size balls, and roll them into mini loaves that are roughly 3 inches long, 2½ inches wide, and ½ inch thick.

Place the loaves on an ungreased baking sheet and set the baking sheet on the middle rack of the oven. Bake for 3 to 4 hours.

Let the loaves cool and then slice.

NOTE: You can experiment with different nuts, seeds, and dried fruits until you find the flavor and texture that you like. This is a very flexible recipe.

ROMAN HONEY CAKE

SERVES 6 TO 8

To ancient Romans, honey was more than a beloved sweet treat (in its honeycomb form) and an ideal sweetener in cooking. To them, honey was magical, offering protection and healing. Many ancient Romans made replica statues and funerary masks using beeswax, believing it would protect them. According to the legendary Roman poet Ovid, these statues also functioned similarly to voodoo dolls—harming the figurine could inflict harm on the human it represented.

Ancient Romans made a wine called mulsum from honey, which they believed aided digestion and promoted longevity. And they often used honey to lift the spirit and dress wounds. Clearly, they were onto something. Honey is known for its antimicrobial properties and for its ability to keep wounds moist and to form a protective barrier on the skin that prevents infections.[10]

We love making this cake for special occasions or when our family craves something sweet. If you can find it, wild local honey is best.

½ cup olive oil

¾ cup wild local honey, plus more for drizzling, optional

1 teaspoon fresh lemon juice

1 teaspoon lemon zest

¾ cup oat milk (or your favorite milk)

1 teaspoon vanilla

1 egg

1½ cups spelt flour

1½ teaspoons baking soda

½ teaspoon sea salt

Whipped cream, optional

Yogurt, optional

Fresh berries, optional

....

Preheat the oven to 350°F and grease a round cake pan.

In a small bowl, beat together the olive oil, honey, lemon juice, lemon zest, oat milk, vanilla, and egg.

In a medium mixing bowl, combine the spelt flour, baking soda, and sea salt.

Gradually add the liquid ingredients to the dry ingredients and beat well.

Pour the mixture into the greased round cake pan and bake for 35 to 40 minutes.

Cool and serve with a drizzle of honey, a dollop of whipped cream, or yogurt and fresh berries, if using.

NOTE: Try pairing this recipe with the Black Fig Jam recipe (page 216).

MASTERS OF WATER AND AIR

How do geese know when to fly to the sun?
Who tells them the seasons?
How do we, humans, know
when it is time to move on?
As with the migrant birds, so surely with us,
there is a voice within, if only we would listen to it,
that tells us certainly when to
go forth into the unknown.

— ELISABETH KÜBLER–ROSS

Our ancestors paid close attention to the unique natural gifts that animals are born with and deemed these traits to be a blessing from the gods. Therefore, the consumption of meat was an honor, and the life of an animal was not taken lightly. It was a ritual, loaded with meaning and symbolism.

For example, migratory birds like geese were seen as magical by most civilizations across Europe, Africa, and the Americas because geese had an innate ability to navigate north and south with the changing of the seasons. Geese were seen as compass-like because of their keen sense of direction, and it was common custom in these culinary traditions to sacrifice a goose with the changing of each season. Four directions, four seasons.

Today the consumption of meat has often become careless, lacking in both humanity and proper ritual—but this wasn't always the way. In Nick's travels while making films all around the world, he's seen that many people still have reverence and respect toward our winged, gilled, and hooved friends.

When preparing meals like those described in this chapter, we keep in mind each act that goes into the acquisition of the meat we use. If we don't feel certain of the integrity of the farm or other source, we look elsewhere. Consciousness, especially with regard to meat, is important.

AL KABSA

One of the oldest known dishes in the Middle East (Saudi Arabia and Yemen, in particular), Al Kabsa is a dish designed to bring communities together. Dinner guests usually sit in a circle on the floor and eat this savory meal, served on a big platter, with their right hand, using a regional flatbread to scoop with. Even though women tend to do most of the cooking in this region of the world, Al Kabsa is so revered that most men also take pride in preparing it.

This recipe features chicken, one of the healthiest animal proteins you can consume. Protein is critical to help your tissue heal and regenerate, especially after an injury or illness. Chicken is also rich in B vitamins (B_6 and B_{12}), selenium (important for immune health), and niacin (helps keep your nervous and digestive systems optimally functioning).

FOR THE AL KABSA

- ¼ cup olive oil
- 1 cup diced red onions
- 7 garlic cloves, minced
- 3 chicken breasts (preferably free range), cut into chunks
- 2 cups uncooked basmati rice
- 1 tablespoon minced cilantro
- 1 teaspoon cardamom seed
- 1 teaspoon ground black pepper
- 1 teaspoon ground cumin
- 1 cup chopped fresh tomatoes
- 2 dried limes,* grated
- 1½ teaspoons sea salt
- ½ cup raisins
- ½ cup sliced almonds

FOR THE SAUCE

- 1 cup chopped fresh tomatoes
- ⅓ cup chopped fresh mint leaves
- 1 teaspoon sea salt
- ¼ cup chopped green chili peppers

*You can find dried limes at Middle Eastern specialty stores or order them online.

In a large skillet, heat the olive oil on medium heat and toss in the onion. Sauté until lightly browned. Add in the garlic and sauté for about 1 minute.

Add the chicken breast and cook for another 5 minutes.

Add the rice, spices, tomatoes, dried limes, and salt, and cook for 5 more minutes, coating the rice in all the juices.

Add enough water to cover all the contents. Bring to a soft boil. Once it's boiling, turn down the heat, cover, and simmer for 30 minutes.

Add the raisins and almonds and cook for an additional 5 minutes.

Remove from the heat.

(CONTINUED)

SAUCE

In a small bowl, combine the tomatoes, mint leaves, sea salt, and 1 to 2 tablespoons of water, enough to give a little juice to the sauce. Add half the mixture to a food processor or blender and pulse for a few seconds. Add the processed mixture back into the bowl and stir to combine.

Serve the Al Kabsa with the sauce spooned over the top.

NOTE: A perfect side dish for Al Kabsa is the Tomato Onion Salad (page 86).

FIRE-ROASTED CHICKEN WITH MAYA ADOBO SAUCE

Contributed by Shannon Kring, Emmy-winning producer/director and cookbook author. Learn more at shannonkring.com.

Hacienda San Lucas is an absolutely magical eight-room eco-retreat located in the mountains overlooking the ancient Mayan ruins of Copán, Honduras, near the Guatemala border. I've had the great pleasure of working alongside its Mayan Chorti cooks, who lovingly handcrafted some of the best food you'll find anywhere. This recipe is adapted from theirs.

I love the Maya adobo sauce on grilled vegetables, vegetable tamales, or herbed rice. I'm a vegetarian, but some swear by the sauce as an accompaniment to steak. Hacienda San Lucas's recipe calls for culantro, a milder-tasting cousin to cilantro, but we'll use parsley instead.

If you prefer not to fire-roast or grill the chicken, feel free to roast it in the oven at 425°F. If you're using the oven, you may wish to cook the chicken in the sauce.

FOR THE FIRE-ROASTED CHICKEN

1 head garlic, cut in half crosswise

1 small yellow onion, cut in half

1 carrot

1 stalk celery

1 whole 7-pound roasting chicken

1 tablespoon unsalted butter

Sea salt, to taste

Freshly ground black pepper, to taste

FOR THE MAYA ADOBO SAUCE

½ cup unsalted butter

3 large yellow onions, chopped

5 cloves garlic, chopped

3 tablespoons creamy peanut butter

3 large jalapeño peppers, grilled and minced

1 medium dried chipotle pepper

1 medium dried ancho chili

3 tablespoons toasted annatto seeds*

1 cup toasted white sesame seeds

1 cup toasted pumpkin seeds

1 pound very ripe pear or grape tomatoes

2 cups chopped cilantro

1 cup chopped flat leaf parsley

2 tablespoons chopped mint

¼ cup chopped fresh thyme leaves

¼ cup shaved Central American or Mexican chocolate

6 basil leaves, thinly sliced (en chiffonade)

Sea salt, to taste

Freshly ground black pepper, to taste

Look for annatto seeds at Caribbean specialty grocers or online.

FIRE-ROASTED CHICKEN

Stuff the garlic, onion, carrot, and celery into the cavity of the chicken. Fold the wing tips under, and tie the legs together loosely. Rub all exposed skin with the butter, and season to taste with salt and pepper.

(CONTINUED)

Roast the chicken on a medium-temperature grill with the lid down, or in the oven at 425°F, until it is golden brown and a thermometer inserted into the thickest part of the thigh registers 180° F, about 90 minutes.

Remove the contents from the cavity, and place the chicken on a platter. Just prior to serving, you can decide whether you'd like to slice the meat or shred it with a fork.

MAYA ADOBO SAUCE

Melt the butter in a large pot over medium heat. Add the onion and garlic and sauté until golden. Stir in the peanut butter.

In a food processor or with a mortar and pestle, grind together the jalapeño peppers, chipotle pepper, ancho chili, and annatto seeds. Add them to the pan.

Stir in the toasted sesame and pumpkin seeds, tomatoes, cilantro, parsley, mint, and thyme. Just before serving, stir in the chocolate and basil. Season to taste with salt and pepper. Skim off any unwanted fat.

PRESENTATION

This dish is lovely served family style. I like to serve the sauce as they do at Hacienda San Lucas, in a terra-cotta pot.

QUECHUA CEVICHE

Did you know that fish can be cooked without using any heat whatsoever? This ancient preparation method for fish gets its name from the Quechua word *siwichi* and is a highly nutritious and adventurous way to eat seafood. About 2,000 years ago, the Moche, a coastal civilization of Peru, began mixing ferments from banana and passion fruit with fish as a method of cooking without fire. The recipe has evolved since then, and now citrus fruits—lemon and lime—are used as the active cooking agent. While the citrus juices and vinegar add great flavor to the dish, their main purpose is to denature the proteins in the fish, resulting in the quasi-cooked end product.

Fish are an important protein source throughout the world. You can use sea bass, trout, or other firm white fish for this recipe. These types, like most fish, provide your body with vital nutrients (including vitamin D). Studies show that eating fish may lower your risk for heart attacks, strokes, and heart disease,[1] may improve brain functioning as you age,[2] and may help prevent depression.[3]

Choose your fish wisely if you are going to attempt this dish, because the ceviche process does not kill bacteria and parasites nearly as well as traditional cooking methods do.

NOTE: If you are concerned about the "rawness" of this dish, try steaming the fish for 5 minutes before adding it to the mixture.

- 2 cups fresh corn kernels
- ½ cup thinly sliced red onion
- ½ cup fresh-squeezed lime juice (approximately 4 limes)
- ½ cup fresh-squeezed lemon juice (approximately 4 lemons)
- ¼ cup fresh-squeezed orange juice (approximately 1 orange)
- 1 tablespoon white vinegar
- 6 to 8 garlic cloves, chopped
- 1 chopped aji amarillo* or habanero pepper
- 2 cups small chunks firm white fish such as bass or halibut
- 2 to 3 cups small to medium shrimp, peeled and deveined
- ¼ cup packed cilantro leaves
- 1 teaspoon salt
- ¼ teaspoon ground black pepper

Try searching grocery stores, co-ops, or farmers markets for these peppers.

Steam the corn until it's just done, 3 to 5 minutes. Drain and set it aside.

Soak the thinly sliced onion in cold water for 10 minutes. Drain.

In a casserole dish, whisk together the lime juice, lemon juice, orange juice, vinegar, garlic, and chopped pepper. Add the fish, shrimp, corn, and onions, and mix together until fully coated.

Cover and place in the refrigerator for 1 hour.

Mix the contents again and return it to the refrigerator for another 2 hours, mixing occasionally. The fish will look "cooked" when ready.

Add the cilantro and season with salt and pepper before serving.

PATARASHCA
(AMAZON ROASTED FISH)

SERVES 4

Coming from a region known for its tremendous diversity of local fish, Patarashca is a native delicacy from the Amazon that has been passed down from generation to generation for thousands of years. This jungle dish is made by taking a whole fish and rolling it in spices and then wrapping it in a banana leaf (or tin foil or corn cob leaves) and placing it on hot coals to cook. Once it's cooked, you unwrap the leaves to reveal a savory, herb-infused fish lover's delight.

This recipe turns to thyme or oregano (or try both) for flavoring and medicinal benefits. It's believed that thyme possesses antimicrobial, anti-inflammatory, antiviral, and antioxidant properties.[4] While oregano is also high in antioxidants,[5] which can help reduce inflammation, this small green herb may help fight off bacteria[6] and viruses[7] too.

- 1 tablespoon olive oil
- 6 tablespoons lemon juice (about 2 lemons)
- 3 tablespoons fresh thyme leaves
- 4 small whole sea bass, trout, or other firm white fish, gutted and scaled
- Salt and pepper, to taste
- 12 thin fresh lemon slices (orange or lime slices can be substituted for variety)
- 4 sprigs fresh thyme or oregano
- 8 large banana leaves, soaked in water, or 8 corn cob leaves, or use tinfoil lightly coated with oil
- 8 toothpicks (soaked in water)

....

In a small mixing bowl, add the oil, lemon juice, and fresh thyme leaves. Mix well.

Season the fish with salt and pepper, and brush both sides of the fish with the lemon mixture.

Lay the lemon slices and thyme sprigs over the top of each fish.

Lay one banana leaf on top of another, forming a cross.

Place a fish in the center of each of the crossed leaves and wrap the fish, securing it with toothpicks.

Place the fish pouches on the grill and cook for 4 to 6 minutes on each side, or roast in the oven at 450°F for 15 minutes.

To serve, place a fish pouch in the center of each plate and remove the toothpicks.

NOTE: Try pairing this dish with the Lemon Quinoa Salad with Hemp Seed (page 89).

NOURISHING PROTEIN PATTIES

SERVES 4

We don't usually think of hamburgers as medicinal, but that's how they may have (partly) risen to fame, at least in the United States. In the mid-1800s, James H. Salisbury, a physician for the Union Army in the Civil War and a researcher, claimed he cured digestive issues in soldiers by feeding them a diet of ground, cooked beef patties. In our era, studies have revealed that while burgers likely won't make the "healthiest foods" list, Dr. Salisbury may have been onto something. Minced beef is more rapidly digested and absorbed than steak, meaning your body receives the amino acids (protein) faster.[8]

While hamburgers have become synonymous with the United States, eating minced meat is not a recent discovery. Early peoples created delicious and nourishing dishes using ground or minced meat for thousands of years. Ancient Romans mixed ground meat with pine nuts, peppercorns, wine, and spices. Kofta, which combines meat such as lamb with various spices, has been found in early Arabic cookbooks.

FOR THE PATTIES

1 pound ground beef (lean) or chicken

3 garlic cloves, minced

1 tablespoon chopped fresh sage

1 tablespoon chopped fresh thyme

1 tablespoon chopped fresh rosemary

1 tablespoon chopped fresh basil

Juice and zest of 1 lemon

1 egg

1/3 cup breadcrumbs

1½ tablespoons olive oil (add only if you're using ground chicken)

1 teaspoon salt

½ teaspoon black pepper

1 tablespoon olive oil

FOR SERVING

Romaine lettuce

Tomato, sliced

Red onion, sliced

Pickles, sliced

4 pitas, whole wheat

Cheese (Romano, cheddar, Swiss, or your choice), optional

....

In a medium bowl, combine all the ingredients and mix thoroughly. Shape into 4 equal-sized round patties.

On a griddle or in a large frying pan on medium, heat 1 tablespoon of olive oil. Add the patties. For chicken: Cook about 3 to 4 minutes per side, until no pink shows. For beef: Cook about 7 to 8 minutes per side for a medium burger. Adjust cooking times based on preference.

Serve in pitas with your favorite toppings. These patties are also great with the Tzatziki Sauce (page 208) and the Oven-Roasted Herb French Fries (page 105).

ANCIENT HERB-MARINATED CHICKEN

SERVES 2

From Egypt to France, Japan to Mexico, the art of marinating meat can be found across continents and throughout time. This cooking technique allowed our ancestors to preserve, tenderize, and flavor meat, which was often in short supply.

This recipe calls for chicken thighs, which in our opinion have gotten a bad rap. As long as you remove the skin, chicken thighs are actually quite nutritious. High in protein and "good" fat, this meat cut is the most tender, affordable, and flavorful (compared to chicken breast, at least)!

We've upped the nutritional profile by using thyme, sage, and mint—three key herbs that herbalists regularly use to promote overall health. Thyme has been shown to help lower blood pressure,[9] and it may help improve mood.[10] Sage is high in vitamin K and the minerals magnesium, zinc, and copper; it also contains antioxidants that may help improve brain functioning.[11] Mint is home to vitamin A and compounds that can aid in helping treat digestion.[12]

Serve this recipe with a salad, on a bun, or with your favorite grain. Try drizzling Tzatziki Sauce (page 208) over the chicken.

- 1 pound boneless, skinless chicken thighs
- 2 tablespoons chopped fresh oregano or 1½ tablespoons dried
- 2 tablespoons chopped fresh thyme or 1 ½ tablespoons dried
- 2 tablespoon chopped fresh sage or 1½ tablespoons dried
- 2 tablespoons chopped fresh mint
- 2 garlic cloves, minced
- 2 tablespoons chopped scallions
- Juice from 1 whole lemon
- 1 tablespoon sea salt
- 1 tablespoon apple cider vinegar
- ⅓ cup olive oil

Lightly pound the chicken thighs with a meat tenderizer.

In a medium mixing bowl, combine all other ingredients. Add the chicken, turn, and coat with the herb mixture.

Cover the bowl and place it in the refrigerator for at least 2 hours, ideally overnight.

In a skillet over medium to high heat, cook the marinated chicken for about 5 minutes on each side.

HERBED SAUSAGE

Long before refrigeration, our ancestors needed ways to store food. Coming from the Latin word *salsus*, meaning "salted," sausages proved to be an ideal way to preserve difficult-to-come-by meat. Throughout the ages and around the world, people have smoked, salted, and made fresh sausages from any animal or fish protein, fat, and spices and herbs transferred into a casing, often made from the animal's stomach lining.

This recipe takes a healthier spin on sausages, opting for the flavoring without all the fat, time preparation, or casings.

Serve the "sausage" on a bun or by itself, crumbled over pasta, or with eggs.

1 pound ground pork or ground chicken

1½ tablespoons chopped fresh thyme or 1 tablespoon dried

1½ tablespoons chopped fresh sage or 1 tablespoon dried

1½ tablespoons chopped fresh rosemary or 1 tablespoon dried

2 garlic cloves, minced

1 tablespoon minced onion

1 teaspoon paprika

1 tablespoon fennel seed

½ teaspoon crushed red pepper flakes

1 tablespoon olive oil

1 teaspoon salt

½ teaspoon black pepper

More olive oil for cooking the patties

In a medium bowl, mix together all the ingredients.

Cover the bowl and set it in the refrigerator for at least 20 minutes or up to 2 hours.

Remove the bowl from the refrigerator and shape the meat into 4 round patties.

Heat some additional olive oil in a medium skillet on medium to high heat, and add the patties. If you're using chicken, cook the first side for about 4 minutes. Flip and cook for another 3 minutes or until the chicken is done (there should be no pink remaining). If you're using pork, cook each side for about 5 minutes or until done (there should be no pink showing).

MEDICINAL CHINESE DUMPLINGS

SERVES 6 TO 8

As the story goes, more than 1,800 years ago, Zhang Zhongjing, the Chinese "sage of medicine," created dumplings to cure villagers of frostbite. To increase the villagers' blood flow, Zhongjing packed mutton, chili, and herbs into a thin layer of dough, sealed it, and then boiled his concoction.

Today we can continue the ancient Chinese tradition of using dumplings as a medicinal herb vessel. This recipe features some of our favorite meat and vegetable fillings that include warming herbs such as garlic and ginger, which can help lower inflammation, aid in digestion, and keep your immune system strong.

This recipe also teaches you how to make gluten-free wrappers. Prepping this dish takes some time, so give yourself at least 2½ to 3 hours in the kitchen to make the dough and shape each dumpling. It's a perfect Sunday afternoon project to do with your family and friends.

But if you're short on time, you can also buy premade dumpling wrappers in the store. Just note that most aren't gluten free.

FOR THE GF WRAPPERS

- 1¼ cups fine white rice flour
- ⅔ cups tapioca starch
- 2 teaspoons xanthan gum
- ½ teaspoon salt
- 3 tablespoons sunflower oil (more if dough is too dry)

FOR THE FILLING

- 1 pound ground pork (it's easy to substitute with firm tofu or seitan)
- 4 ounces shrimp, minced
- ½ cup chopped scallions
- 2 garlic cloves, minced
- 2½ tablespoons minced ginger
- ½ cabbage head, shredded
- 1 teaspoon soy sauce
- 1 tablespoon toasted sesame oil
- 1 egg

FOR THE DIPPING SAUCE

- 1 teaspoon rice wine vinegar
- 2 tablespoons soy sauce
- 1 teaspoon sesame seeds
- 1 teaspoon toasted sesame oil
- 1 teaspoon honey dissolved in 1 tablespoon water
- 1 teaspoon minced garlic
- 1 teaspoon minced fresh ginger

FILLING

Combine all the filling ingredients in a medium bowl.

Mix together and cover the bowl with plastic wrap. Place in the fridge until you're ready to use it. (This filling also makes a great patty for Asian-inspired burgers.)

DIPPING SAUCE

Combine all the dipping sauce ingredients in a small bowl.

Whisk together and put this off to the side while you cook the dumplings.

(CONTINUED)

DUMPLINGS

In a medium bowl, whisk together the rice flour, tapioca starch, xanthan gum, and salt.

In a separate bowl, whisk together ¾ cup of hot water and the oil. Then pour this into the flour mixture.

Mix the contents together with a fork until fully combined.

Dump the mixture onto a lightly floured (with rice flour) cutting board and knead it with your hands into a smooth dough.

Cut the dough into 4 or 5 equal pieces. Form these individual pieces into balls and then tightly wrap each ball in plastic wrap.

Take one dough ball and remove the plastic wrap. Place the ball between 2 pieces of plastic wrap on the cutting board. (This is key because the plastic wrap will prevent the dough from sticking to the roller or the cutting board.)

Using a small rolling pin, roll out the dough to a little less than ⅛ inch thick.

Peel back the top plastic layer and press a circular glass cup upside down into the dough, making 1 test dumpling first. Remove the dumpling from the dough and hold it in your hand. It should be thin enough that you can fill it without breaking it. If it's too dry or thick, reroll the dough ball and add more oil, 1 teaspoon at a time.

Once the dough is rolled out and ready, use the circular glass cup and make as many circular cuts as you can get out of each piece of dough. Reshape any scrap dough into another ball and repeat this process until all of your dough has been used. **Important:** Place your circular dough wraps on a separate plate and cover them with a damp paper towel to keep them moist.

(CONTINUED)

Carefully pick up one wrapper and place about 1 teaspoon of the meat filling in the middle. Fold the wrap over onto itself, creating a half circle, and press down on the open edges to seal it. There are multiple ways to seal the edges—all of them work and taste equally delicious. Here are a few different techniques you can use: 1) Pinch the wrapper in half at a point in the middle. And then fold the skins over twice on each side. In the end it will resemble a little fan. 2) Use a fork to crimp the edges. 3) Fold the wrapper in half, thoroughly press the edges together to create an airtight seal, then use the palm of your hand to flatten the dumpling so it sits upright.

Once your wrappers are all filled and sealed, heat a medium skillet on medium-high heat. Add enough vegetable oil to cover the bottom of the pan and then a little more.

When the skillet is hot, place your first dumpling batch into the pan and cover with a splash guard to prevent grease splatter. Cook for 3 minutes, or until the bottom of each dumpling is light brown.

Carefully add ½ cup of water or broth to the pan and cover it with a glass or metal lid. Lower the heat to medium and cook until the liquid has evaporated.

Place the finished dumplings on a separate plate and continue this process until all pieces have been cooked.

Serve the dumplings with a small ramekin of the dipping sauce.

NOTE: These dumplings can also be steamed using a simple steaming basket.

MEDICINAL CHINESE DUMPLINGS MANY WAYS

Dumplings are the perfect vehicle for many herb and ingredient combinations.
These are two of my favorite dumpling fillings. Use them to stuff the dumpling dough (above).

VEGETABLE DUMPLINGS

½ cup chopped bok choy

½ cup chopped maitake mushrooms

2 teaspoons fresh grated ginger

2 garlic cloves, minced

2 scallions, green parts thinly sliced

1 bunch of spinach, chopped

1 shredded carrot

1 cooked and mashed Yukon Gold potato

1½ tablespoons sesame oil

....

In a small skillet over medium heat the sesame oil and sauté all the ingredients until softened, about 3 to 5 minutes. Cool completely.

TOFU PEANUT DUMPLINGS

1 pound firm tofu, drained and finely chopped

¼ cup chopped peanuts

½ cup chopped scallions

2 garlic cloves, minced

2 ½ tablespoons minced fresh ginger

½ cabbage head, shredded

2 teaspoons soy sauce

1 egg

....

Heat a large wok or skillet over medium-high heat. Add 1 tablespoon oil and allow it to heat, then add the ginger and sauté for 30 seconds.

Add the tofu, seitan, and cabbage and cook for 2 minutes, until just tender. Add the garlic. Gently stir-fry for 1 minute.

Turn off the heat and add the scallions and soy sauce. Taste and season with salt and pepper as needed. Transfer to a bowl and allow to cool. Stir in the egg to bind the ingredients. Add two teaspoons of filling to each wrapper.

NOTE: You can freeze the wrappers before you've filled them. Cut out the wrappers and place them individually on a baking sheet lined with parchment paper. Place the tray in the freezer for 2 to 3 hours or until the wrappers harden. Then place the wrappers in a freezer-safe bag or container. Store for up to 3 months.

DRIED AND CURED WITH CARE

*Travelers had known since prehistoric times
how to provision themselves
when they were away from home.*

— REAY TANNAHILL

Since time immemorial, our ancestors have wandered the world searching for food, water, and shelter. What did they take with them to maintain their energy and stamina when hunting, foraging, or traveling? Long before sandwiches, energy bars, or refrigeration were invented, early humans used one ingenious technique to ensure their food stores would last and easily slip into a pouch or pocket.

Since at least 12,000 B.C. (and probably much longer ago), our ancestors used the power of the sun, salt, and/or smoke to dry and cure just about everything from fruits and mushrooms to fish and game. Considered to be one of the oldest cooking techniques known to humankind, dehydrating food allowed our ancestors to preserve ingredients for weeks and to have quick and highly nutritious meals on the go.

It's not just one civilization that dried and cured food—anthropologists have found evidence of this ancient method scattered across the globe. The First Peoples in North America made pemmican, an early energy bar that often included dried bison, fat, nuts, and fruit. The ancient Romans leaned on sausages to feed their vast military units. In Northern Africa and in the Nile Valley, early humans often dried meat, including camel, goat, and cattle, with spices and herbs. Travel back in time and you'd also find this practice used in China, Persia, and northern Europe.

Many civilizations also believed that dehydrating food had medicinal value. The ancient Chinese believed that dried foods were more nutritious because they contained that ingredient's "true essence." Herbalists and folk healers also regularly dried herbs and spices, mushrooms, and other plants. These ingredients lasted for up to two years, and some people believed that drying generated more potency.

CREE PEMMICAN

French fur traders willing to brave the deep interior of pre–European settlement North America had no choice but to befriend, or at least form a working relationship with, the indigenous tribes who controlled the waterways. In this "business relationship," many customs were exchanged between the two cultures. Among the most useful bits of wisdom passed from the First Peoples to the French was a technique for grinding dried fruits, smoked meat, nuts, seeds, and fat into cakes that would keep indefinitely. This early preserved food—known as pemmican—made it possible for small trading parties to push deep into unknown territories without needing to hunt or gather food for days.

This recipe packs a protein wallop. It calls for a dried or smoked lean meat like bison or turkey, and dates, raisins, and walnuts to give you healthy carbohydrates and fat. The balance between protein, carbohydrates, and fat makes pemmican an ideal go-to snack when you need a quick energy burst.

2 cups chopped smoked or dried bison, turkey, or other lean meat (or for vegans, 1½ cups powdered tofu jerky)

1 cup dates

1 cup raisins

¼ cup wild honey, plus 2 tablespoons

1 cup walnuts

Put all the ingredients except the 2 tablespoons of honey in a food processor (or use a large mortar and pestle). Grind the ingredients together on medium speed, adding the 2 tablespoons of honey little by little at 1-minute intervals. Keep grinding until the mixture is fully mashed and the consistency resembles an energy bar.

Scoop the contents onto a large pan, flatten with a spatula or rolling pin, and slice into bars with a knife.

Refrigerate for 5 hours. Remove the bars from the pan and serve. When prepared correctly pemmican will keep for weeks without any further refrigeration.

AZTEC GRANOLA BARS

SERVES 6 TO 8

In ancient times, divine inspiration and prayer were mixed into every part of daily life, and food was no different. As a symbol of respect, the Aztecs, who lived in Northern Mexico, created miniature figurines of their gods using the tasty and pliable mixture of honey and amaranth. These edible sculptures would be eaten as a type of communion with the higher powers.

The granola recipe below is extremely nutritious, yet the ritual of creating miniature symbols of gratitude out of the pliable ingredients is what our family loves most about it.

Amaranth is considered a super grain that the Aztec, Incan, and Mayan civilizations cultivated. It's rich in manganese, which is important for brain health and the nervous system, metabolizing carbohydrates and fat, absorbing calcium, and regulating blood sugar. Amaranth also contains magnesium, a mineral that plays a huge role in energy production, and studies show that it may have an anti-inflammatory effect.[1]

3 teaspoons coconut oil, divided

½ teaspoon salt, divided

¼ cup amaranth, divided

¼ cup prewashed quinoa, divided

½ cup coarsely chopped dried apricots

½ cup coarsely chopped raisins

1 cup coarsely chopped dried pepitas (pumpkin seeds)

¼ cup honey

¼ cup maple syrup

....

Preheat the oven to 350°F. Line a 9-inch-square pan with parchment paper and lightly grease with coconut oil (about 1 teaspoon).

Heat a large skillet over medium-high heat. Add ½ teaspoon of the coconut oil, ¼ teaspoon of the salt, ⅛ cup of the amaranth, and ⅛ cup of the quinoa, just enough to cover the bottom of the pan with a single layer. Stir the grains with a wooden spoon as they pop, for about 30 seconds to 1 minute. As amaranth grains pop, they change from dark yellow to white, while quinoa grains turn a toasted brown color. Watch them carefully to avoid burning. Once they're popped, remove the mixture from the heat and transfer it to a plate to cool. Be sure to allow the grains to cool before using.

Repeat the process for the second batch, adding ½ teaspoon of the coconut oil, ¼ teaspoon of the salt, and the remaining amaranth and quinoa.

In a medium mixing bowl, add the cooled quinoa, amaranth, chopped fruit, and pepitas. Mix in the honey, maple syrup, 1 teaspoon coconut oil, and remaining salt.

(CONTINUED)

The mixture should be very pliable and easily shaped into symbols, figurines, and letters. Keep the sticky sculptures relatively flat, like a gingerbread man.

Once you've shaped your granola, place the bars onto the parchment paper–lined pan. Using the back of a lightly greased spatula, press firmly on the granola to flatten it.

Bake the granola in the oven for about 15 minutes, or until each shape turns golden brown. Remove from the oven and cool completely before eating.

Store the bars in an airtight container, between layers of waxed paper. These should keep for up to 1 week.

NOTE: To turbo-boost your bars, add 1 tablespoon of maca powder and 1 tablespoon of cacao powder to the mixing bowl along with the quinoa and amaranth.

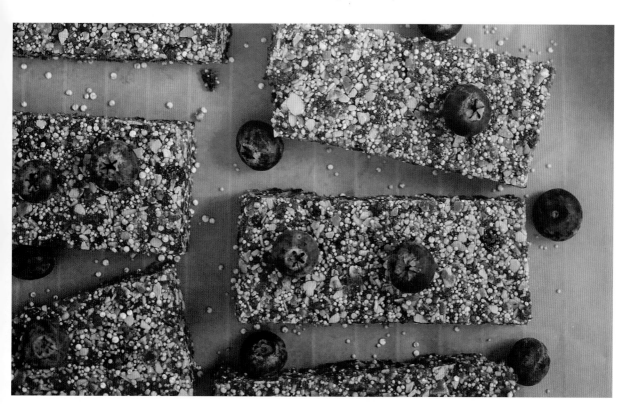

TARAHUMARA ENERGY BAR

SERVES 4

For over 3,500 years, the chia seed has been a nutritional wonder. It gets its name from the Mayan word for strength. The chia seed was so prized for its medicinal value by Mesoamerican civilizations that it was routinely mixed with most treatments, because it was believed these tiny seeds enhanced the patient's ability to absorb medicine.[2]

Just 2 tablespoons of these tiny seeds provide you with some impressive nutrition. They contain considerable protein, including nine essential amino acids, and loads of fiber—more than quinoa, flaxseed, and amaranth.[3] It's believed that chia seeds can help prevent cardiovascular diseases and diabetes.[4]

The recipe below comes from the Tarahumara, indigenous people of Mexico whose name means "to walk well." Interestingly, the Tarahumara, who still exist today, are known for more than walking. They can run extremely long distances without stopping (50 to 100 miles at a time). These super athletes do this for fun, not for competition. This recipe is their traditional energy bar.

1 cup ground cornmeal	2 tablespoons wild honey
1/3 cup chia seeds	1 teaspoon ground cinnamon

Preheat the oven to 365°F and lightly grease a cookie sheet.

In an ungreased skillet, cook the cornmeal on medium heat for 5 to 10 minutes, until light brown.

Pour the browned cornmeal (also called pinole) into a mixing bowl, adding the chia, honey, cinnamon, and enough water (about 1/3 cup) to give the mixture a thick batter-like consistency. Mix until fully combined.

With a large spoon, place individual scoops of the batter onto the cookie sheet.

Bake for 15 minutes or until the bars are crispy.

NOTE: This is a great baseline recipe that you can add other ingredients to. Try using pumpkin seeds or sunflower seeds if you want to bulk it up a bit.

BEAN, SEED, AND HERB CRACKERS

SERVES 6

From ancient Egypt to Mesopotamia to the great Indus civilization, humans have consumed flat, unleavened breads, whether baked in ovens, grilled over hot coals, or fried in oil. Around the Middle Ages, twice-baked breads—also known as biscuits—became popular. Combining flour with water and salt, biscuits were first baked and then slowly dried out in the oven. This technique helped preserve food and became a staple for people such as explorers and soldiers who were undertaking long voyages. From the biscuit, crackers were created. Physicians believed these thin, crispy, dry, and usually unsweetened flat breads were easy on the stomach and could help ease stomachaches and nausea.

This recipe uses chickpea flour, which compared to wheat flour contains twice the amount of folate (B_9), fewer calories, triple the amount of fiber, and more protein. It also calls for ground flaxseed, one of the oldest crops and a powerhouse nutrient-rich food too. Flaxseed is high in thiamine, a B vitamin that's essential for energy levels and metabolism, and it has omega-3 fatty acids, which help boost brain functioning and may reduce risks of cardiovascular diseases and inflammation.[5]

6 tablespoons ground flaxseeds

2 cups chickpea flour

1 teaspoon salt

3 tablespoons dried rosemary

1 tablespoon dried thyme

6 fresh sage leaves, chopped

1 teaspoon garlic powder

1 teaspoon onion powder

2 tablespoons sesame seeds

2 tablespoons olive oil

Flaky salt to garnish

....

Preheat the oven to 350°F. Line a baking sheet with parchment paper.

In a small bowl, combine the flaxseeds with 1 ¼ cup of water. Set aside.

In a medium bowl, mix the chickpea flour, salt, and herbs. Add the olive oil and additional 4 tablespoons water. Mix until well combined. The batter should be thin.

Transfer the batter onto the baking sheet. Spread it out evenly with a spatula.

Sprinkle the sesame seeds and flaky salt on top.

Bake for 15 to 20 minutes until golden.

Cool completely before breaking into crackers.

CACAO BITES

Few foods have been as revered as the cacao bean and the date. The Olmecs, Mayans, and Aztecs of Mesoamerica all roasted and ground the cacao bean into powder to make pastes and drinks. They believed cacao was a "gift from the gods," and besides using it in food and drinks, they believed that the cacao bark, oil, leaves, and flowers were effective for burns, gastrointestinal issues, cuts, mental fatigue, fever, and increased virility. Research suggests that cacao may help lower blood pressure,[6] as well as improve blood flow to the brain, thus boosting functioning,[7] stabilizing moods, and reducing symptoms of depression.[8]

Across continents and time, dates were also used for food and medicine. They held religious significance as well. The three major religions of Islam, Judaism, and Christianity believe dates are significant. Judaism even regards this sweet fruit, native to the Middle East and Africa, as one of the seven holy foods. Ancient physicians used the fruit, leaves, flowers, and seeds of the date palm in tonics and concoctions as an aphrodisiac and to treat wounds, urinary and liver issues, bronchitis, and fever. Today science has shown that dates may have disease prevention properties that lower risks of cancer, inflammation, tumors, and diabetes.[9]

1¼ cups chopped raw walnuts

1¼ cups unsweetened shredded coconut

2 cups Medjool dates

½ cup cacao powder

⅓ cup maca powder

½ cup chopped goji berries

1 tablespoon melted coconut oil

2 tablespoons maple syrup

½ teaspoon sea salt

Flaky salt to garnish

Combine all ingredients in a food processor.

Line a baking dish with parchment paper and pour in the mixture. Sprinkle flaky salt on top.

Refrigerate for at least 2 hours.

Slice into small squares and store in the refrigerator for up to 2 weeks.

OVEN-DRIED KALE CHIPS

SERVES 6

The process of dehydrating fruits, vegetables, and meats most likely began as an accident. We've all left food out for too long before, and oftentimes this results in something quite unappetizing. But imagine the delight a Sumerian farmer might have felt when they came upon a fig or date that was left out in direct desert sunlight for a few days: a delicious new flavor profile would emerge and, most importantly, a food that could be stored in bulk for months.

While kale chips aren't exactly an ancient food, this hearty, healthy leafy green is, and so is the ancient technique of dehydration. We've been taught that "chips" aren't always the healthiest choice, but using kale flips the script. Even when they're slowly roasted in the oven, kale chips don't lose their nutritional value, so you'll still get their beneficial fiber, antioxidants, vitamin A and C, calcium, B vitamins, and potassium.

In this recipe, we use nutritional yeast, which contains all nine amino acids, making it a complete protein and a popular go-to ingredient for vegans. Nutritional yeast also has lots of B vitamins, including B_{12}, which help improve energy and metabolism.

⅔ cup cashew butter

⅓ cup nutritional yeast

2 tablespoons onion powder

1 tablespoon garlic powder

½ teaspoon sea salt

⅔ cup oat milk

Juice of 1 lemon

2 bunches kale

....

Preheat the oven to 250°F.

Cover two baking sheets with parchment paper.

In a blender or food processor, add all ingredients except the kale. Purée until thick and creamy. Set aside.

Tear the kale leaves away from the stalk in 2- to 3-inch pieces. Discard the stalks and place the leaves in a large bowl.

Pour the purée over the kale. Use your hands to toss the kale pieces so the purée covers each piece.

Spread the kale onto the two baking sheets. Make sure each piece is flat and does not touch or overlap other pieces.

Bake for about 40 to 45 minutes. Check regularly to ensure the kale doesn't burn and is dehydrating.

Remove from the oven. Allow to cool completely before eating.

TIMELESS TRAIL MIX

Humans have combined dried fruits and nuts for millennia. In Iran and other Persian-influenced countries including Azerbaijan, Afghanistan, and Tajikistan, they often eat a mixture called ajeel on Yaldā Night, which celebrates the winter solstice and the turn from darkness to light. Ajeel might feature pistachios, dried mulberries, roasted chickpeas, pumpkin seeds, and raisins.

This recipe features a dried fruit, nut, and seed medley. Inca berries, also known as golden berries, are native to South America and were once reserved for royalty in Peru. They're high in antioxidants, potassium, protein, and vitamins B, C, and A. We've also added goji berries, a fruit that comes with fiber, iron, and vitamins A and C. Plus we've added pumpkin seeds, which are filled with antioxidants, vitamin K, phosphorus, manganese, magnesium, zinc, and copper. And we've thrown in walnuts, the nut with the most omega-3 fatty acids. Walnuts have also been found to increase the good bacteria in the gut[10] and support good brain functioning.[11]

2 cups dried Inca berries

2 cups dried goji berries

2 cups dried mulberries

2 cups raw pumpkin seeds

2 cups raw cacao nibs

½ teaspoon sea salt

1 cup walnuts

1 cup toasted coconut flakes

....

Combine all ingredients in a large bowl.

Store in an airtight jar or container.

BITTER, BRINY, AND BOLD

As one eats kimchi, one eats the universe,
and in so doing becomes part of the universe
and the universe becomes part of man.

— KOREAN PROVERB

Long before refrigeration, humans turned to the ancient art of fermentation to preserve their foods. And while today we often link pickles and sauerkraut to Germany, the true origin of these ferments lies much farther east and many years back. Most historians consider China to be the birthplace of fermentation, and it's believed that the ancient Babylonians were turning cucumbers into pickles as far back as 5000 B.C.

By leaving vegetables and milk on the counter too long, we've all accidentally started our own ferments. This is very much how humans first stumbled across the miracle of fermentation—through accident and happenstance.

But what led early tribes to continue to replicate the mistake? Were these bitter, briny, and bold creations embraced simply for their flavors, or did early humans immediately recognize the practical, nutritional, and healing value of fermented food? Perhaps it's a bit of everything.

SACRED SAUERKRAUT

SERVES 4

While most commonly associated with bratwursts and hotdogs, sauerkraut—which is fermented cabbage—is said to date back as far as 700 B.C. It's believed that laborers working on the Great Wall of China discovered the dish when they began storing shredded cabbage in rice wine in order to keep the cabbage long after its growing season ended. Legend has it that the great Mongolian warrior and ruler Genghis Khan brought sauerkraut to Europe.

Involving a fermentation process similar to what's used to make pickles and kimchi, sauerkraut elevates the nutritional profile of fresh cabbage into one that's a true powerhouse for healing. Fermenting cabbage makes it more easily digestible and its nutrients more quickly available to the body. This sour dish is filled with vitamins C, B, and K, fiber, and probiotics, which are terrific for the gut microbiome. Many popular folk remedies also use sauerkraut to help heal cold sores and boost the immune system. Like most ferments, sauerkraut contains numerous beneficial probiotics that help keep your gut microbiome healthy. Some studies have found that sauerkraut contains 28 distinct probiotic strains[1] and a variety of enzymes that support your body in breaking down food.[2]

This recipe calls for spring water. If you use water containing fluoride or chlorine, it will affect the ferment.

1 medium red cabbage
1½ tablespoons sea salt
1 teaspoon dill seed
Juice of 1 lemon

Spring water (enough to submerge)
2 mason jars

....

Using a large kitchen knife, slice the cabbage in half and remove the core. Place each cabbage half on its flat side and carefully shred into thin strips. Alternatively, you can grate the cabbage using a box grater. When you're finished, place the shredded cabbage into a large ceramic or metal mixing bowl.

Add the sea salt, dill, and lemon juice to the mixing bowl and use your hands to combine the ingredients. Squeeze and knead the cabbage shreds to soften them. Let the mixture sit for 30 minutes.

Using a serving spoon, scoop the cabbage mixture into the mason jars, leaving 2 inches of room at the top. Pour the spring water on top of the cabbage. There should be a line at the top of the mason jars indicating how high to fill them with spring water.

Drizzle a final bit of lemon juice over the exposed surface at the top of the jar. This will prevent the growth of any unwanted bacteria during the fermentation process.

FERMENTATION

Seal the jars and place them in a shady storage space that always stays at room temperature. The fermentation process can take between 4 and 10 days.

(CONTINUED)

Make sure to "burp" each jar every few days. To do this, simply unscrew the lid and let the effervescence release and then place the lid back on.

After 4 or 5 days, start sampling the sauerkraut daily until it has reached the flavor and consistency you desire. Once you feel it has reached perfection, serve it or place it in the fridge.

This ancient probiotic-rich food will keep fresh for months.

NOTE: For extra flavor, try adding a tablespoon of fresh thyme or rosemary to your sauerkraut mixture before securing the lid.

KOREAN KIMCHI

SERVES 8

Kimchi is a traditional fermented vegetable dish that originated in Korea more than 3,000 years ago. Like other ferments, kimchi provided Koreans with a way to preserve food through the harsh winter. Unlike its cousin sauerkraut, this classic dish usually includes chili peppers (heat level varies) and other seasonings, including ginger and garlic, and features different vegetables, including cabbage, cucumbers, or radishes. It's allowed to ferment for a few days, or sometimes underground in jars for months. As Korea's national dish, kimchi can be found in everything from pancakes to stews and soups and can be enjoyed as a side dish or with rice. Studies suggest that eating kimchi may help support your immune system (like most ferments),[3] prevent yeast infections,[4] and lower inflammation levels.[5]

This recipe is great for people new to making kimchi and for anyone looking for a solid, basic recipe to experiment with. Once you've grown comfortable with the fermenting process, you can play with the taste—add or reduce salt, try different spice combinations, and even add other vegetables like cucumbers for variety.

4 tablespoons sea salt

1 pound Chinese cabbage (napa or bok choy), coarsely chopped

1 daikon radish or a few red radishes, sliced*

1 to 2 carrots, sliced

1 to 2 onions, chopped

3 to 4 garlic cloves, minced

3 to 4 red chilies, seeds removed, minced

3 tablespoons (or more) grated fresh ginger

A quart-size (liter) jar

*Look for daikon radishes at health food stores or Asian specialty food stores.

In a large bowl, create a brine by mixing about 4 cups of water and the 4 tablespoons of sea salt. Stir well to thoroughly dissolve the salt.

Add the cabbage, radish, and carrots to the brine. Cover with a plate or other weight to keep the vegetables submerged until they're soft. Let them soak for a few hours or overnight.

Process the onions, garlic, red chilies, and ginger in a food processor or use a mortar and pestle to mix into a paste.

Drain the vegetables, reserving the brine. Taste the vegetables. If they seem too salty, rinse them under water. If you cannot taste the salt, sprinkle the vegetables with a couple more teaspoons of salt and stir thoroughly.

Mix the vegetables with the onion-garlic-chili-ginger paste and the reserved brine. Stir to combine, and then fill a quart (liter) jar to the top. Pack the vegetable mixture tightly into the jar, pressing down until the brine rises.

(CONTINUED)

Ferment the kimchi at room temperature (at 65 to 70° F) for 1 to 4 days or in the refrigerator for 2 to 3 weeks. Taste the kimchi every day to check for desired sourness. The ingredients should be well blended, and you shouldn't be able to identify individual ingredients.

Once it has fermented and reached your desired flavor and consistency, store the kimchi in the refrigerator, where it will continue to slowly ferment. Make sure liquid always covers the vegetables. Kimchi should stay fresh for up to 6 months.

NOTE: Save some of the juice and sediment from your first batch of kimchi to use as a starter culture for the next batch you make.

THE MESOPOTAMIAN PICKLE

SERVES 8

It's believed that pickling food may date as far back as ancient Mesopotamia in 2400 B.C. Ancient Romans made a concentrated fish pickle sauce called garum from leftover pickling brine, while it's been said that Cleopatra credited a steady diet of pickles for her good complexion.

Often made with cucumbers, pickles are a good source of fiber, and when eaten in moderation (they do contain salt), can aid in digestion. Some of the fresh herbs used in pickling brine, such as fresh garlic, turmeric, dill, and mustard seed, also help boost the immune system.

NOTE: Make sure not to use cucumbers that have a wax coating on them—this will disrupt the pickling process.

1 gallon freshly picked pickling cucumbers

2 large bulbs garlic, all cloves peeled

2 big bunches dill, roughly chopped

1 small piece horseradish root

3 to 4 tablespoons pickling spice (allspice, mustard seeds, cloves, bay leaf, black pepper, etc.)

6 to 7 tablespoons unrefined sea salt, divided

A 1-gallon thoroughly cleaned glass jar with lid

Make sure your pickling cucumbers are thoroughly scrubbed and clean and then soak them in chilly water. This helps perk them up before the fermenting begins.

In a large mixing bowl, toss the cucumbers, garlic, dill, horseradish, and pickling spice together.

Scoop the mixture into the 1-gallon jar in 4-inch increments, adding a bit of sea salt in between each cucumber layer until you've used the whole tablespoon.

In the now empty mixing bowl, prepare a brine of 6 tablespoons of unrefined sea salt to 2 quarts of spring water and vigorously mix until the salt is fully dissolved.

Pour the brine into the jar with the pickles until all are submerged in the salt water. Cover with the lid.

Allow your ingredients to sit for 5 to 7 days, tasting them occasionally to see if you're happy with the amount of fermentation that has occurred. If your pickles aren't fully ready by then, leave them for a few additional days.

Once you're satisfied with the flavor, transfer the jar to the refrigerator. The pickles will keep for up to 6 months.

YOGURT (LABAN)

SERVES 16

The word *yogurt* originated in Turkey over 1,000 years ago. Like many inventions, yogurt was discovered by chance. Over 8,000 years ago, herdsmen on the plains of central Asia began the practice of milking their cows. They stored their yield in a traditional liquid container made from the lining of cows' stomachs. The natural enzymes of the stomach-lined containers curdled the milk, making something similar to yogurt.

The benefit of this newfound dairy food was that it kept longer than milk and it tasted great. Little did the early herdsmen of Mongolia, Siberia, and China know that what they stumbled upon through sheer happenstance would become a staple to many great civilizations to come, including the Greeks, the Romans, the Egyptians—and, well, us.

Yogurt contains many health benefits, including protein, calcium, B vitamins (particularly B_{12} and riboflavin), phosphorus, magnesium, and potassium.

1 gallon cow or sheep milk

4 tablespoons plain yogurt that contains live or active cultures (yogurt starter)

A large glass bowl with a lid

A heavy bath towel

....

In a large saucepan, warm the milk on low to medium heat until it forms a skin.

Remove the milk from the heat and allow it to cool to 110°F.

In a small bowl, mix the yogurt starter with ⅓ cup of the hot milk until it's smooth in consistency.

Pour this mixture into the rest of the milk, stirring well with a wooden spoon.

Pour all contents into the large glass bowl and cover it with the lid. Wrap it securely with the towel and store it in a warm place for 6 hours.

Remove the towel and the lid and refrigerate the bowl. Once chilled, it will firm up. It should last in the refrigerator for up to 2 weeks.

NOTE: If you want thicker yogurt, just let it sit for an extra day or so until it reaches the desired texture.

SUPERFOOD YOGURT BOWL

SERVES I

Our bodies need proper fuel to process emotions, heal tired tissues, and ward off disease. But when we're stressed, it's easy to forget to eat or to eat too much—neither of which helps keep our bodies strong and healthy. This recipe features ingredients that help support and nurture your body and mind during stressful times.

The goji berry, also known as the wolfberry in China, is said to help strengthen the body, boost the immune system, and prolong life.[6] This small reddish berry, considered both a fruit and an herb, has been used for more than 2,000 years in Traditional Chinese Medicine. Coconut shavings may help nourish and protect the brain.[7] Greek yogurt contains probiotics that help the gut microbiome, and granola brings fiber.

½ cup plain Greek yogurt (or plant-based equivalent or use the homemade yogurt recipe on page 180)

½ tablespoon goji berries

½ tablespoon coconut shavings

¼ cup granola

....

Mix all ingredients together in a bowl.

Enjoy immediately or seal in an airtight jar overnight to let the granola soak up the moisture from the yogurt.

ETHIOPIAN INJERA

This delicious North African staple is used as both a tasty bread wrap and a serving dish. The main ingredient used to make injera, called teff, is one of the oldest grains eaten by humans. In ancient Egypt the grain was so revered that the pharaohs were buried with it as a symbolic "last meal." Rich in protein, complex carbohydrates, and good fats, injera is a healthy bread substitute by today's standards.

The fermenting action in this dish comes from the yeast that is added, combined with a rather long "sitting" period of 2 days.

In traditional Ethiopian cuisine, a thin 3-foot injera cake is spread out on the table with various vegetables, sauces, and meats portioned in mounds across it. Dinner guests eat only with their hands, tearing off bits of the injera from the edge and using it to scoop up the food spread over the top. While it isn't practical to make a 3-foot injera in your home kitchen, you can easily adapt by using the largest pan you own.

You might like to try incorporating some of the following dishes as toppings: Roasted Winter Roots (pg. 97), Mustard Greens Bhutuwa (pg. 17), Greens in Groundnut Sauce (pg. 23), and Traditional Berber Tagine (pg. 61).

½ cup teff flour*

½ teaspoon active yeast

½ teaspoon local honey

Pinch of sea salt

Pinch of black salt

2 teaspoons olive oil

Find teff flour in health food stores or online.

....

In a large mixing bowl, whisk together all the ingredients. Place a lid over the bowl and let it sit for 2 days on a countertop. After 2 days, remove the lid and drain off any water that has formed on the surface.

Whisk together the teff batter once more until fully combined.

Place a large pan with a tight-fitting lid over medium to high heat and add the olive oil. Use a cloth or napkin to evenly distribute a light coating of the oil across the surface of the pan. You don't want excess oil for this recipe.

Much like making a pancake, ladle the teff batter into the pan, tilting it to evenly distribute the batter across the bottom.

Wait 1 to 2 minutes for small bubbles to begin forming on the top and then cover the pan tightly with the lid. After 3 to 5 minutes the injera should be fully cooked through the center.

Remove the injera from the heat, place it on a heated plate or cookie sheet, and repeat until no batter remains.

Enjoy your delicious injera for up to 5 days once cooked.

NOTE: Don't be alarmed at the slightly vinegar-like aroma of the finished injera. This is part of the fermentation process and is quite good for digestion.

HERBAL KOMBUCHA

SERVES 6 TO 8

This fizzy tea has become a superstar in the health and wellness world because, when consumed daily, kombucha helps heal the gut, regulate bowel movements, and boost immunity. Likely originating in China, this fermented tea has become widely enjoyed throughout the world.

Like other ferments, kombucha is actually easy to make at home. And the magic starts with SCOBY. Shorthand for symbiotic cultures of bacteria and yeast, SCOBYs are rubbery, pancake-like living cultures that eat the sugars in the tea blend, turning it into the amazing antioxidants, vitamins, and probiotics that kombucha is well known for.

The first step to making kombucha at home is to find a SCOBY. You can get your SCOBY (and the liquid it came in) from a trusted natural food retailer or a kombucha-crazed friend.

The second step is to prepare your tea. You can put together any combination of healing herbs and flavors you love, as long as you add the proper amount of sugar. You'll need 1 cup of sugar for every gallon of tea (do not use honey).

- 2 tablespoons green tea leaves
- 1 gallon filtered water
- 1 cup sugar
- 2 tablespoons* dried herbs of choice (Some good options are peppermint, holy basil, lemon verbena, and chamomile.)

- 1 SCOBY
- 1½ cups starter liquid that the SCOBY came in
- A 1-gallon glass jar (or other sealable glass vessel)
- Cheesecloth or a tea towel

*If using two different herbs, add 1 tablespoon of each.

In a medium pot, bring the water to a boil and add the tea leaves along with the dried herbs. Reduce to a simmer and cook for 5 minutes.

Add the sugar and stir until dissolved.

Strain out all loose herbs. Allow to cool for at least 30 minutes.

Add the tea and sugar mix to the jar. Place the SCOBY on top. Add the starter liquid. Cover with the cheesecloth.

Place in a dark, clean cabinet where no critters or light can damage the brew. Wait 2 to 3 weeks.

Taste test: The kombucha should be slightly acidic, but sweet. It should be a little bubbly, but not overly. When your kombucha tastes right, you can decant it into smaller bottles. This tea should yield a nice peppermint and/or holy basil taste with the bitterness of green tea. It should last for 6 to 8 weeks.

NOTE: Be sure to save the SCOBYs (there should be two now, if you've done it right) when your kombucha is ready to be bottled. Store it in a sealed container in the refrigerator. It will go dormant and can last for up to 6 months.

SHAMANIC FIRE CIDER

SERVES 6 TO 8

Apple cider vinegar is a jack-of-all-trades ingredient that brings your body back into homeostasis by introducing healthy bacteria to your microbiome, which largely controls the health of your immune system. When you add more healing herbs to the mix—like garlic, ginger, turmeric, horseradish, cayenne, and other goodies—you get a strong (and delicious) wellness shot that prevents illness and shortens your recovery time if you're already feeling sick.

Our dear friend and world-renowned herbalist Rosemary Gladstar created fire cider in 1981. She then taught her apprentices and students how to make this spicy elixir. Fire cider eventually became popular across the country and is now a staple in herbalists' pantries worldwide.

Because of its immune-boosting properties, it's the perfect drink to make in the fall and winter to ward off colds, the flu, and other pathogens.

¼ cup grated horseradish (fresh or jarred)

¼ cup finely chopped onion

⅛ to ¼ cup finely chopped garlic cloves

⅛ cup grated fresh turmeric

⅛ cup chopped or grated ginger

2 sprigs fresh rosemary

1 cinnamon stick

Calendula, optional

Cayenne (fresh or dried), optional and to taste

2 cups raw, unpasteurized apple cider vinegar

¼ to ½ cup honey, warmed

A 1-quart glass jar

....

Place all the vegetables and herbs in the 1-quart glass jar.

Pour in enough apple cider vinegar to cover all the vegetables and herbs by 2 inches. Cover the jar opening with waxed paper. Screw on the top, and shake it up!

Place the jar in a cool, dark place for at least 4 weeks. Strain out the dregs so that you're left with only the liquid.

Warm your honey, which helps it mix with the cider. Add the honey to the jar and stir together. Refasten the lid and store the fire cider in your refrigerator.

Take 1 teaspoon per day to prevent illness or 1 tablespoon per day if you show symptoms of a cold/flu.

NOTE: Cut and leave your garlic exposed to the air for 10 to 15 minutes. This increases the compound allicin, which has a variety of health benefits, including protecting the heart, lowering blood pressure and cholesterol, reducing oxidative stress in the brain, and fighting viruses and bacteria.[8]

CELTIC DRUIDS HONEY MEAD

SERVES 8

Honey mead, also known as "honey wine," has been enjoyed for thousands of years. According to Maguelonne Toussaint-Samat, author of *A History of Food*, "It [mead] can be regarded as the ancestor of all fermented drinks." Even the earliest known fermentation, dating back to 9000 B.C. in northern China, contained honey. Archaeologists have found remnants of mead-making spanning Europe, Africa, and Asia.

Mead, which is made by fermenting honey and water with yeast, was often infused with medicinal herbs to make a metheglin, or spiced mead. The medicinal brew would be prescribed to treat a variety of illnesses, depending on which herbs it contained.

This is a basic, very traditional mead recipe that uses warming spices such as cloves, ginger, and cinnamon, known to aid digestion.

NOTE: Try to use a native honey from your area that was made from various flowers, bushes, and trees. This will give your mead more nutrients and flavor.

¼ cup fresh ginger root

6 whole cloves

1 cinnamon stick, broken into pieces

2 lemon peels

Juice from 2 lemons

3 pounds wild honey (about 48 ounces)

1 ounce baker's yeast

EQUIPMENT

A large stock pot

A thermometer

A 2-quart fermentation jar with airlock (available in any brewing store)

3 750-millileter amber glass hock bottles

Muslin cloth

Smash the ginger with a mallet to semi-crush. Tie the ginger, cloves, cinnamon stick, and lemon peel in a muslin cloth and place it in the stock pot. Add 16 cups of water and the lemon juice, and bring the mixture to a boil.

Once the mixture is boiling, remove it from the heat. Allow the contents to cool to 120°F and then drizzle in the honey. Allow the mixture to cool to 70°F. Remove the muslin bag containing the ginger and lemon peel. Crumble the yeast into the honey water and stir gently.

Pour the liquid (this is called the "must") into the fermentation jar (it should reach about three-quarters full) and fit the airlock. Leave the must for 2 weeks or until all fermentation has finished. Rack if necessary. (Racking means siphoning the liquid from the original container into a fresh one, leaving any unwanted sediment behind.)

After 2 weeks, pour the contents into the three bottles, seal, and store. The mead is ready for consumption after 4 to 6 months, but is best kept for several years!

ENCHANTING SPICES AND SAUCES

*Each spice has a special day to it. For turmeric it is
Sunday, when light drips fat and butter-colored
into the bins to be soaked up glowing, when you
pray to the nine planets for love and luck.*

— CHITRA BANERJEE DIVAKARUNI

Spices have long been employed for medicine and food. The prevailing theory is that using spices for culinary purposes began the same way many cooking techniques did—accidentally. In order to transport meat, hunters gathered leaves and twigs to use for protective wraps. During the trip home, the aromatic wrapping materials would season the meat, functioning as a primitive marinade. Over time, the more flavorful wrappings, or herbs, were noted and sought after. Thus began the saga of spice that quickly grew in value as trade routes between Asia and Europe opened.

There is an abundance of anecdotal evidence indicating early human use of herbs and spices for their *healing effects* as well. Recently discovered cuneiform tablets from around 3000 B.C. tell a detailed story of the popular spices of ancient Mesopotamia. Some of the essential herbs and spices from that era include thyme, sesame, cardamom, turmeric, saffron, poppy, garlic, cumin, anise, coriander, silphium, dill, and myrrh. The Babylonians actually prayed to a medicinal god of the moon who influenced the potency of healing herbs. Part of this tradition included the harvesting of herbs by moonlight so as not to damage their medicinal qualities with the harsh sun. In India, medicinal herbs have been used for thousands of years with a richly documented history. Some of India's favorite culinary and curative spices include cinnamon, cardamom, ginger, turmeric, and pepper. Traditionally, cardamom and cloves were wrapped in a betel nut leaf and chewed after meals to aid digestion. Various combinations and herbal preparation methods are outlined in Ayurvedic medicine and strictly adhered to by devout practitioners.

We also see spices interwoven in many religious and spiritual practices throughout the ages. The Bible mentions frankincense, coriander, cumin, and myrrh. In many shamanic cultures, from Australia to Siberia, shamans (priests/healers) burned or brewed different spices (and herbs) to invoke a trancelike state so they could travel to the spiritual world to gain important information for their tribe or to heal a community member.

Humankind's culinary, medicinal, and spiritual need for spices has driven us to the ends of the earth, and it was a major catalyst in leading explorers to discover the new world. Our love of zest didn't stop during the age of exploration—it continues flourishing today.

BERBERE SPICE

Berbere spice is a blend of herbs originating in Ethiopia and Eritrea. This unique mixture is used in many Ethiopian soups or stews. Aside from its distinct flavor, berbere features one of our favorite medicinal herbs: fenugreek.

Fenugreek is one of the oldest known medicinal herbs and has been used to help treat various health issues, such as appetite loss, constipation, bronchitis, insomnia, diabetes, hormone imbalances, and cancer. Traditional Chinese Medicine labeled fenugreek a "phlegm remover," and some cultures believe that consumption of the seeds improves sexual function in men and increased milk flow in nursing mothers. A poultice containing fenugreek seeds mixed with warm water was traditionally used to relieve muscle pain and reduce swelling. This herbal blend can be used in curries and other spicy dishes.

½ teaspoon ground fenugreek seeds

½ cup whole dried chilies (ancho, amarillo, serrano, and you can also blend them)

¼ cup paprika

1 tablespoon salt

1 teaspoon ground ginger

1 teaspoon onion powder

½ teaspoon ground cardamom

½ teaspoon ground coriander

¼ teaspoon ground nutmeg

¼ teaspoon granulated garlic

⅛ teaspoon ground cloves

⅛ teaspoon ground cinnamon

Grind the chilies into a powder, then add all the ingredients to a small bowl and mix with a fork until well combined.

GARAM MASALA

Garam masala is a spice blend often found in curries and soups and used as seasoning for lentils, meat, and fish. It's believed to have originated in northern India. Garam means "hot" and masala means "spices." While the seasoning blend and proportions often differ from family to family throughout India, garam masala usually features aromatic, ground spices such as coriander, cumin, cloves, cinnamon, nutmeg, and black pepper.

In the ancient Hindu medicine system, Ayurveda, it's believed that garam masala warms and heats the body, which aids in metabolism and digestion. When digestion is sluggish, it's thought that toxins accumulate in the body. Studies suggest that eating a meal seasoned with garam masala does speed up digestion.[1]

4 tablespoons coriander seeds

2 tablespoons cumin seeds

1 tablespoon whole black peppercorns

2 teaspoons cardamom seeds from about 15 pods, measured after removing and discarding the husks

3 inches cinnamon stick

1 teaspoon whole cloves

1 whole nutmeg

In a small pan, roast one spice at a time until they are fragrant, about 1 minute each. Immediately remove the spice from the pan and place it on a plate to cool. In a spice or small coffee grinder, combine all the spices and grind to a fine powder.

Transfer the mixture to a glass jar with an airtight seal. The garam masala will keep indefinitely.

NAM PRIK PAU

This Southeast Asian chili condiment is a pillar of Thai cooking. The preparation is simple, and the applications for this chili pepper relish are almost infinite. The chili pepper itself is actually native to the Americas, with records indicating its cultivation almost 6,000 years ago. This spicy veggie was considered sacred to the ancient Mayans of Central America.

The Portuguese brought the chili pepper overseas to Asia in the 1600s, where it was quickly embraced by the culinary centers in the port cities. It now has a place at the table in most Thai homes and restaurants.

Nam Prik Pau is a delicious addition to soups, salads, eggs, stir-fries, and stews.

5 red chili peppers (substitute with ground red pepper, but don't use cayenne—it's too spicy)

½ cup coconut oil

4 large garlic cloves, minced

4 shallots, minced

2 tablespoons lime juice

6 tablespoons brown sugar

4 tablespoons fish sauce

1 teaspoon tamarind paste

2½ teaspoons shrimp paste

Remove the stems from the chili peppers and chop them into small pieces.

In a medium skillet or saucepan, cook the chili peppers without oil on high heat. Stir constantly so the peppers don't burn. After about 10 minutes, the peppers should become crispy and brown. Remove from heat.

In a small spice or coffee grinder, grind pepper pieces to a fine powder.

In a small saucepan, heat the coconut oil on medium heat. Sauté the garlic and shallots until lightly browned.

Remove the saucepan from the heat, and separate the garlic and shallots from the oil, placing them into a small bowl.

In a food processor, combine the garlic, shallots, lime juice, brown sugar, fish sauce, tamarind paste, shrimp paste, 4 tablespoons of water, and the chili powder and blend until it forms a paste.

(CONTINUED)

In the saucepan, add the paste to the coconut oil and simmer on low heat. Stir constantly until you reach the desired texture and taste. For a thinner consistency, stir for about 5 to 7 minutes. For a thicker sauce, simmer for about 8 to 10 minutes. Remove from the heat and let the paste cool.

Pour the oil mixture into a small jar. The Nam Prik Pau will keep for about 4 months if refrigerated.

HEAL-ALL GARLIC AND OLIVE OIL INFUSION

MAKES 1 CUP

One of the first dishes Nick ever learned to make was this recipe, which his Italian grandparents taught him. Featuring Mother Nature's heal-all power herb, garlic, this recipe is the perfect way to reap its medicinal and antioxidant benefits.

Garlic is one of the oldest crops that humans have intentionally grown. Ancient Sumerians (in the region we know today as south-central Iraq) used garlic to treat a variety of ailments as far back as 2600 to 2100 B.C. In ancient India, China, and Egypt, garlic was also hailed as a powerful cure for depression, cough, parasites, high blood pressure, stomachaches, constipation, respiratory tract diseases, and weakness. Ancient Egyptians even served garlic to their slaves to make them stronger and able to work longer.

Modern science has shown that our ancestors were right to utilize garlic as a healing aid. The major active compound in garlic is allicin, which gets enhanced when the bulb is either crushed or chopped. Allicin from garlic has proven to be antibacterial and antiviral,[2] making it a natural remedy that helps ward off germs. Garlic appears to boost the immune system, increasing white blood cell production—the very cells that fight off infections.

On top of its immunity-boosting benefits, garlic shows promise as an antioxidant, fighting inflammation, which can lead to heart disease, cancer, and other chronic diseases; lowering cholesterol and blood pressure; and reducing the risk of heart disease.[3]

The best way to reap garlic's medicinal and antioxidant benefits is to eat it raw (in small amounts). In its raw form, garlic also offers many prebiotic properties, which help feed the good bacteria in your digestive system, keeping your gut in optimal health.

However, not everyone is up for the pungent, spicy garlic challenge, so adding raw garlic to dips, dressings, and toppings is easier on your taste buds. In our home we use this recipe in many ways. We add a spoonful to the top of pasta dishes, soups, and salads. Once it's fully refrigerated, you can also spread it cold across your favorite type of toasted bread.

(CONTINUED)

3 large garlic cloves, minced

1 cup olive oil

1 glass gar, with a lid
(10 to 12 ounces is ideal)

....

Break each garlic bulb into its separate cloves and carefully peel off the skins.

Blend the garlic in a small food processor until fully minced. (You can also use a kitchen knife and mince by hand.)

Transfer the minced garlic into the empty jar.

Pour olive oil over the top of the garlic all the way up to the top.

Fasten the lid on the jar. Turn the jar over a few times to fully combine the olive oil and garlic.

Refrigerate after each use.

HA SIKIL PA'AK

MAKES 2 CUPS

The name Ha Sikil Pa'ak is Mayan for "water, pumpkin seed, tomato," but this delicious vegan dip is much more than that. When you first taste this well-spiced and creamy delight, it may appear to include a rich dairy product, but Ha Sikil Pa'ak is 100 percent vegetable based and has been that way for the better part of a millennium. Not only that but this Mesoamerican schmear is extremely nutritious and is an old go-to for enhancing fertility in women.

Pepitas (raw pumpkin seeds) are believed to improve prostate and bladder health,[4] and they are one of the best sources of magnesium, which may help control blood pressure,[5] reduce the risk of heart disease,[6] and maintain healthy bones.[7]

4 medium tomatoes

1 cup pepitas (raw, shelled pumpkin seeds)

1 bunch scallions, chopped

½ cup chopped cilantro

¼ cup fresh lemon juice

1 pinch crushed red pepper

Salt, to taste

....

Turn on the broiler to high.

Slice each tomato into sixths and place the pieces on a lightly oiled baking sheet. Transfer the baking sheet onto the top oven rack and broil for 5 minutes, or until the tomatoes are lightly charred on top. Remove the pan from the oven.

Transfer the tomatoes to a food processor and add the remaining ingredients. Blend on high for about 1 minute, or until the contents have a thick creamy texture.

Transfer the mixture to a medium bowl and chill in the refrigerator for 1 hour, or until ready to serve.

Serve with crisp vegetables or traditional tortilla chips.

DANDELION PESTO WITH PINE NUTS

Pesto has ancient roots in Rome, where basil, garlic, olive oil, pine nuts, grated cheese, and salt were blended to create a sauce. But if you travel the Mediterranean region, you'll find variations on this classic dish. Walnuts or almonds instead of pine nuts. Sweet red peppers and tomatoes instead of basil. Pecorino cheese instead of Parmesan.

The beauty of pesto is that you can create any combination your taste buds desire. This recipe leans more traditional but uses an often-overlooked ingredient—dandelion greens—in lieu of basil. It also adds a splash of lemon juice to brighten the flavors.

1 large bunch Italian flat leaf parsley

2 cups chopped dandelion greens

½ cup pine nuts

½ cup olive oil

Juice of ½ lemon

3 large garlic cloves

3 tablespoons Parmesan cheese (if you're a vegan, nutritional yeast is a good substitute)

Sea salt

....

Fill a medium saucepan with water and bring to a boil.

Add the parsley and dandelion leaves to the pot, making sure everything is fully submerged. Blanch for 1 minute. Strain the water from the saucepan, leaving the greens in the pot. Immediately fill the saucepan with cold water to halt the cooking process.

Strain the greens and transfer them into a blender or food processor.

Add the pine nuts, olive oil, lemon juice, garlic, cheese, and a pinch of sea salt to the greens and blend until the pesto reaches the desired consistency.

CHIMICHURRI

Historians believe that roasting meat was the first cooking method humans ever discovered. It stands to reason that flavoring meat with herbs and spices wasn't far behind. Chimichurri is a great example of how you can take healing herbs to create an elixir-like sauce to use over any meat-based dish, especially those that are grilled or roasted. Thought to have originated in Argentina and Uruguay as an accompaniment to meat dishes—especially steak, empanadas, and sausages— chimichurri is a thick, chunky sauce that's more like a salsa.

Some of our favorite ways to eat chimichurri are with proteins, vegetables, pastas, stews, rice dishes, or roasted potatoes.

2 cloves garlic, minced

⅓ cup olive oil

2 tablespoons finely chopped fresh oregano

2 bunches fresh parsley, finely chopped

2 tablespoons apple cider vinegar

1 teaspoon crushed red pepper

1 teaspoon salt

Combine all ingredients in a mason jar and store in the refrigerator for up to 7 days.

TZATZiKi SAUCE

Our son's best friend is a picky eater. One night when he came to dinner, his mom warned us that he'd probably push his food around, so we shouldn't take it personally. But something magical happened that evening, and we credited it all to the flavor explosion that is tzatziki sauce. We served this recipe with the Ancient Herb-Marinated Chicken (page 145) and Oven-Roasted Herb French Fries (page 105), and not only did our son's friend clean his plate but he also asked for seconds!

Variations on this dish can be found throughout Greece, Turkey, and other parts of the Middle East. But the base—yogurt mixed with herbs—remains the same.

This recipe calls for coconut yogurt, which, like most yogurts, is rich in probiotics. It also features dill, which contains vitamins A and C, and manganese, an essential mineral that plays a crucial role in supporting the brain, nervous system, and metabolism.

1 large cucumber, peeled and roughly chopped

1 cup coconut yogurt, plain, unsweetened (you can also use regular yogurt)

1½ tablespoons minced fresh dill or 1 tablespoon dried

1 tablespoon minced fresh mint

1 garlic clove, grated

Juice from ½ lemon

1½ tablespoons olive oil

½ teaspoon sea salt

Finely chop the cucumber in a food processor.

In a medium bowl, combine the cucumber with all the remaining ingredients. Mix well and place in the refrigerator to chill.

Use as a dipping sauce with vegetables, or drizzle over any protein or Fertile Crescent Falafel (page 81).

FENNEL SYRUP

Making a flavored honey syrup is one of the easiest ways to incorporate healing herbs into your diet. Fennel is usually our go-to. This licorice-flavored herb native to the Mediterranean was revered by ancient Greeks and Romans, who used it in cooking and medicinally. Fennel also holds a storied place in the ancient healing practices of Ayurveda and Traditional Chinese Medicine. Today herbalists use fennel to aid digestion, ease menstrual pain, and prompt breastfeeding in nursing mothers.

Try adding this to tea or drizzling it over oatmeal or yogurt.

2 tablespoons fennel seeds   ½ cup water
¼ cup honey

Crush the fennel seeds with a mortar and pestle or in a spice grinder.

Add the fennel to a saucepan and cover with ½ cup of water.

Bring to a boil and then lower to a simmer and warm for at least 30 minutes, or until the liquid has reduced by half.

Strain out the seeds and pour the liquid back into the saucepan.

Heat the liquid to lukewarm and then add the honey. Stir until the honey melts.

Keep refrigerated.

HONEY DIJON DRESSING

Today we commonly think of apple cider vinegar as the perfect addition to salad dressings (because it is!), but long ago, ancient humans sought out this lip-puckering liquid for its numerous healing properties. In 400 B.C. the father of modern medicine, Hippocrates, treated common colds and coughs by mixing apple cider vinegar with honey. In 1958 Dr. D. C. Jarvis, a family physician from Vermont, wrote the book *Folk Medicine*, which focused on remedies that generations of Vermonters had used to remain healthy and heal illnesses. Apple cider vinegar ranked high on Dr. Jarvis's folk remedies.

Recently some small studies have found that apple cider vinegar may help lower blood pressure,[8] aid in weight loss,[9] and reduce cholesterol and triglycerides,[10] plus it may have antifungal[11] and antibacterial properties.[12]

This recipe comes from Nick's mother's restaurant, Plain Jane's, and was always a hit. She used to heat it up in small ramekins for patrons to use as a dipping sauce, drizzle over a bed of spinach with dried cranberries and nuts, or pair with grilled chicken.

1 cup mayo (we like to use avocado mayo, but any kind works)

2 tablespoons spicy mustard

2 tablespoons honey

1 tablespoon apple cider vinegar

2 tablespoons olive oil

Salt, to taste

....

In a small bowl, whisk together all the ingredients.

If you want a thinner consistency, add a little water.

This zesty dressing is amazing as a dipping sauce, for proteins, or over salad. It will keep in the fridge for up to 3 weeks.

NOTE: If possible, use raw apple cider vinegar, which contains "the mother." The raw form hasn't been pasteurized, so it contains more beneficial bacteria and yeasts.

SPICY HERBAL HONEY

From Europe to the Americas to Asia and Africa, hot peppers have found their way into the diets of humans for thousands of years. Crushed red pepper flakes are a mixture of multiple dried red peppers, including cayenne pepper.

This recipe marries spicy with sweet. Use it drizzled over pizza, as a dip (especially on a cheese and/or charcuterie board), or in a marinade for chicken or steak.

1 cup honey

4 teaspoon crushed red pepper flakes

¼ teaspoon cayenne pepper

In a small saucepan on low heat, combine all the ingredients. Bring to a simmer and cook for 10 minutes. Do not let the mixture boil.

MORABA 'YEH ANJIR
(BLACK FIG JAM)

MAKES I CUP

The fig is considered one of the oldest fruits eaten by humans. Tales of the fig show up just about everywhere, including in major religions. Under the fig tree the Buddha found enlightenment. The wolf mother of the twin founders of Rome—Romulus and Remus—rested under a fig tree after giving birth. In southern Arabian times of old, giving the fig sign (making a fist and putting your thumb through the index and middle finger) was a way to ward off evil. Mohammed's followers called the fig tree "the tree of heaven."

What made the fig so special? Perhaps it's because, as modern science is uncovering—and confirming—it offers some unique medicinal benefits, including anticancer and antimicrobial properties, as well as helping the liver, boosting blood sugar levels, and aiding gut health.[13]

NOTE: Try spreading this over the Roman Honey Cake (page 129).

1 pound fresh, ripe black or green figs

1 cup raw sugar

2 teaspoons lemon juice

2 teaspoons rose water

1 teaspoon ground cardamom

Sterilized mason jars

....

Clean the figs and remove the stems.

Puncture the figs until they each ooze their juices (it is important to use ripe figs).

Place the figs in a mixing bowl along with the sugar, and cover the bowl with a lid. Shake the bowl vigorously for 2 minutes, until each fig is completely coated with sugar.

Place the bowl in the refrigerator overnight, allowing the figs to release some of their juices, which will comingle with the sugar to create a delicious syrup.

The following day, remove the lid and pour the contents into a medium pot. Stir constantly over low heat until the mixture bubbles.

Add the lemon juice and continue to gently stir and cook for 30 minutes more.

Before removing the pot from the stove, add the rosewater and ground cardamom.

Using a large serving spoon, scoop the figs and syrup into the jars. Clean the rims with a cloth and seal the lids. Place the jars in the refrigerator.

The jam may take a few days to set and will keep in the fridge for up to 2 months.

TIME-TESTED TEAS AND TONICS

If you ask Zen people they will say tea is not something that you pour with unawareness and drink like any other drink. It is not a drink, it is meditation; it is prayer. So they listen to the kettle creating a melody, and in that listening they become more silent, more alert.

— BHAGWAN SHREE RAJNEESH

Tea drinking is an ancient tradition with a somewhat tangled timeline. Most experts agree that the craft of making and drinking tea likely had its beginnings in Yunnan, China, around 1500 B.C. (Shang Dynasty). However, boiling herbs in water to create a flavorful and medicinal drink was probably quite common in human enclaves stretching back before the Mesopotamian era. The Chinese, however, perfected the art of brewing tea, and through the ages this steamy and curative beverage has become entwined in rich mystical traditions and ceremonies.

You could fill an entire book with the various creation stories of how tea came to be. The following theory is one of our favorites because it shares the same "accidental happenstance" scenario that we've seen in many of the other recipes in this book. Legend has it that around 2750 B.C. Emperor Shennong was outside enjoying a cup of hot water (which in those times was a common practice for health reasons), when a few leaves from a nearby tree fell into his cup and steeped into a delicious medley. After enjoying his pleasantly restorative cup of pre-tea, Shennong began experimenting with the practice of immersing dried leaves in hot water, thus giving birth to modern-day tea craft.

Legend and myth aside, the teas included in this chapter have proven healing properties that have withstood the test of time and the harsh scrutiny of modern science. When you prepare them with care and attention to both inner and outer environmental factors, very few things in this world are quite as nourishing to the soul.

TIP: Never use aluminum utensils or containers for your tea extractions because aluminum reacts with acidic fruits, vegetables, and herbs at high temperatures—potentially contaminating your food. Glass, porcelain, silver, and Pyrex are best!

REISHI TEA

Known as "lingzhi" or "mushroom of immortality" in China, reishi has been used as a healing medicine for over 7,000 years. In the early years reishi was available only to the ruling class, but now we commoners can partake of its legendary healing benefits. Although known for its powerful anti-tumor activities[1] and potential blood pressure regulating properties,[2] reishi might best be thought of as an immune modulator.[3] As opposed to other medicines that "boost" your immune system, this wonder mushroom can help train your immune system to work more effectively.

On a spiritual level, elders say that reishi "cools" the heart and allows us to see life challenges in a new light. Sages are said to drink this sacred concoction daily for its profound consciousness-opening properties. Traditional Chinese Medicine is centered around balancing the energy systems of the body, and reishi is one of the master herbs used to accomplish this.

3 ounces dried reishi mushroom

1½ quarts spring water

Honey, to taste (optional)

Milk, to taste (optional)

....

Dried reishi is extremely hard. To soften it, soak it in water overnight. The next day you should be able to cut it into small pieces.

Drop the reishi pieces into an open pot filled with the spring water, cover the pot with a lid, and boil slowly for 1 to 2 hours.

To serve, carefully pour just the tea into cups and add honey and/or milk.

A pot of reishi tea can be kept in the refrigerator for a week.

NOTE: Reishi pieces can be boiled again, so reserve yours to make another batch.

SEVEN SUPER HERBS PERFECT FOR A SIMPLE TEA

Healing often lies in simplicity. There is nothing more simple and potentially potent than tossing herbs into a cup or teapot and letting them steep in hot water for 20 minutes to 2 hours. Physicians and healers have prescribed these ancient remedies for thousands of years, and you can reap the benefits too. These seven super herbs are ideal to leave soaking in water, allowing the liquid to extract many healing properties.

1. Ginger
2. Dried chamomile flowers
3. Mint
4. Lemon balm
5. Motherwort
6. Sage
7. Pine needles

HOLY BASIL ELIXIR

In Ayurvedic medicine, holy basil is classified as a *Rasayana*, an herb that promotes overall health and boosts longevity. For 3,000 years, tea from this herb has been prepared daily and is believed to help balance the chakras, or energy centers, in the body.

Known as *tulsi* in India, holy basil is referred to as the "elixir of life" and can be found growing around the most revered Hindu shrines and temples. Aromatic and delicious, this fix-all has found its way into many surrounding cultures, including those of Southeast Asia and the Middle East.

The herb has withstood the scrutiny of science as well. Holy basil is rich in antioxidants; is extremely detoxifying; regulates the adrenal system, making it an effective anti-stress tonic; and possesses unusually high levels of the essential fatty acid alpha-linolenic acid, which is an anti-inflammatory.[4]

¼ teaspoon fennel seeds

¼ teaspoon ground cumin

½ teaspoon ground cloves

⅓ teaspoon green cardamom, crushed

1 to 2 teaspoons fresh or dried holy basil (tulsi)

Place all ingredients along with a cup of water in a small pot and simmer for 20 minutes.

Strain the ingredients and then pour the tea into a mug or cup and enjoy.

HOMEMADE COCONUT MILK

YIELD: 2 CUPS

We love adding a splash of coconut milk to the Holy Basil Elixir on the previous page. While you can buy this at the grocery store, you can also make your own. Here's a quick recipe that pairs perfectly with this tea.

| 1 cup coconut water | 2 dried figs |
| ½ cup coconut meat | |

Mix all the ingredients in a blender for 1 minute. Pour the contents into a nut milk cloth bag and squeeze the liquid into a separate container. Discard the solids. Once the Holy Basil Tea is ready, pour the contents through a strainer into serving cups. Add coconut milk to taste.

Before taking your first sip, breathe in the wafts of wellness from this ancient beverage.

ALMIGHTY HONEY

Honey and tea have a long history together. Herbalists and folk medicine practitioners have turned to honey and tea to help fight colds, loosen mucus in the chest, soothe a sore throat, and warm the body.

Honey is easy to digest, helps stave off allergies (if it's consumed in its raw, local form), has no preservatives or additives, tastes delicious, and if properly stored can be kept indefinitely.

No wonder reverence for this sticky gold turns up in the written and painted history of almost *every* human tribe and civilization in recorded history. In the Old Testament of the Bible, Israel was referred to as "a land flowing with milk and honey." The sacred writings of India and Egypt mention honey. The pharaohs were buried with it. John the Baptist ate it along with locusts, and in ancient Rome and around the world, honey was often used to heal wounds.

According to a myth of the Cheyenne (a North American plains indigenous tribe), the first men lived on honey and wild fruits and were never hungry. In Hebrew the word for bee is *dbure*, stemming from *dbr*, which means "word." The ancient Hebrew texts refer to honey as "the truth" because it's perfect in its original form, needing no refinement.

Even collecting honey has long been considered a divine miracle. In the Vedas—the ancient Sanskrit texts that are both early Indian literature and the first scriptures of Hinduism—honey is considered an actual god. The ancient Mayans also believed bees were "godsends," hailing from a sacred hive in the middle of the earth, and sent to awaken humans from laziness and apathy. Myths of a divine cavern guarded by bees also exist in Greek mythology; young Zeus's birthplace was a cave guarded by swarms of fiery bees. And the temple of the Egyptian god Osiris was also known as "the mansion of the bee."

Why does every pocket of sophisticated human existence hold a special place in the pantry for this sweet and fragrant goo? Five words come to my mind: holy, ancient, healthy, medicinal, and preservable.

Raw honey contains the most beneficial healing properties. You can find it at most health food stores or online. Try adding a dollop of honey to any of the tea recipes in this chapter. If possible, use raw or unpasteurized honey.

TIBETAN RHODIOLA TEA

SERVES 4

Grown at altitudes of 11,000 to 16,000 feet above sea level, the rhodiola is a cactus-like plant with a bright red flower. Its bark is widely used in places like Tibet and Siberia to make this delicious, cinnamon-colored curative tea. It's said that since the beginning of their civilization, Tibetan monks used this ancient sacred herb to strengthen their spiritual power.

The main ingredient in rhodiola is glucoside, which has been shown to improve cognitive function and sexual function, as well as alleviate fatigue and depression.[5] Also rich in flavonoids, amino acids, and bionutrients, this tea has been used for centuries to cope with the cold Siberian climate and a stressful lifestyle. To this day it is said in Siberia that people who drink rhodiola will live to be 100.

2 tablespoons rhodiola roots

2 wide-mouth quart jars (mason jars work perfectly)

1 fine mesh strainer

2 tablespoons raw honey, optional

....

Place the rhodiola roots into the jars.

In a large pot with a lid, bring 8 cups of water to a boil and then cool slightly.

Pour the water over the roots, cover loosely, and allow the tea to steep for 10 to 15 minutes. Strain.

If you're adding honey, wait until the tea has cooled a bit and then add it to the jars, cover, and shake well.

PINE POLLEN TEA

Ancient Chinese healers were always on the hunt for herbs that would give everlasting longevity and strengthen the life force or "qi" (energy) in the body. Pine pollen made the list. The Xin Xiu Ben Cao (Tang Materia Medica) is believed to be the first Materia Medica of China, and this index goes into great detail about the miraculous healing effects that can be gleaned from pine pollen. It was so revered for its life-enhancing properties that ancient cultures gave this seasonal tree essence the nickname "longevity powder."

For over 2,400 years, pine pollen has been put to great use in China, but it only recently gained a following in the West. It's said to be particularly beneficial for regulating the immune system, protecting the liver, and lowering blood sugar, and for its anti-inflammatory, anti-aging, anti-fatigue, anti-tumor, and antioxidant properties.[6] Pine pollen also has A, D, E, and B vitamins; minerals such as zinc, copper, iron, calcium, and magnesium; and essential fatty acids.

1 tablespoon pine pollen

2 teaspoons maca

¼ teaspoon ground cinnamon

....

In a large pot, heat 2 to 3 cups of water to nearly boiling. Drop in the pine pollen.

Steep for 10 minutes.

Stir in the maca powder and cinnamon.

MAYAN HOT CHOCOLATE

SERVES 3

Chocolate has been with us for a very long time. At an ancient excavation in northeast Guatemala, vessels were discovered that contained residue of cacao seeds (raw chocolate) that date back to 480 A.D. and earlier. The scientific name of the chocolate plant, *Theobroma*, translates literally to "food of the gods," and to early Mesoamerican civilizations that is exactly what it was. In Mayan society, everyone—rich and poor alike—enjoyed a frothy, rich, and delightfully bitter beverage made from this sacred seed. Consumed at most meals, the chocolaty drink was quite different from our European hot chocolate; it was thick and rich, often with a head of fatty cocoa butter foam, and the cinnamon and spice deepened the flavor and gave you a little kick.

The Mayans celebrated an annual festival every April to honor their cacao god, Ek Chuaj, which included animal sacrifices, feathered costumes, burning incense, and exchanging gifts. Because of its powerful aphrodisiac properties, Mayan couples also drank the sacred beverage for engagement and marriage ceremonies.

The flavanols found in cacao have been found to increase blood flow to the brain, which can help improve cognitive performance.[7] Cacao may also reduce stress and promote feelings of relaxation and calm,[8] and improve blood pressure and skin, dental, cardiovascular, and respiratory health.[9]

2 tablespoons raw cacao powder

½ teaspoon cornstarch (this is a thickening substitute for the high-butterfat milk content used by the ancient Mayans)

¼ teaspoon ground cinnamon

⅛ teaspoon ground nutmeg

¼ teaspoon ground chili powder

1 cup sheep or cow's milk or almond milk

Honey (optional)

....

In a small mixing bowl, combine cacao, cornstarch, and spices.

Add 1 tablespoon of the milk and whisk the mixture into a paste.

In a medium saucepan over medium heat, slowly warm the remaining milk, stirring occasionally so the milk doesn't stick to the bottom. Before the milk comes to a boil, remove the pan from the heat and slowly add the paste, stirring to combine.

Return the saucepan to the stove and bring the mixture to a simmer, stirring constantly until thickened, about 5 minutes.

Pour into a mug and add honey to the desired sweetness.

HERBAL COFFEE ALTERNATIVE

SERVES 1

For many folks, the best part of waking up is a warm cup of joe. Coffee drinking has become so embedded in our culture that we don't think twice about it. But when it comes to optimizing our health and happiness, it's sometimes worth examining the habits that we take for granted. When we look to the past, we find that our ancestors weren't daily coffee drinkers. Instead, they used it (and caffeine) sparingly, opting to serve it during ceremonies or to honored guests.

Thankfully, there are some equally amazing coffee alternatives that we can use to stoke our energy and cognitive clarity. This recipe features guayusa, the Amazonian holly species that gives us the caffeine punch but at much more manageable levels than coffee does. A cup of guayusa tea contains approximately half as much caffeine as a cup of coffee. A relative of yerba maté, guayusa is also loaded with antioxidants and other beneficial compounds that have been found to improve moods and alertness.[10] Guayusa also contains triterpenoids that have antihyperglycemic effects, meaning it may help stabilize blood sugar levels.[11]

1 to 2 teaspoons dried guayusa leaves

1 teaspoon powdered chaga extract

1 teaspoon cacao powder

Dash of vanilla extract

Pinch of sea salt

¼ teaspoon ground cinnamon

Touch of honey, optional

Splash of your favorite milk, optional

....

Put the guayusa in a tea ball or infuser and drop it into your favorite mug. In the same mug, add the chaga, cacao, vanilla, salt, and cinnamon.

Pour boiling water over the tea blend and steep for 5 to 7 minutes.

Remove the tea ball or infuser and pour the mixture into a blender. Add a touch of honey and a splash of milk, if desired.

Blend on medium speed for 10 seconds.

Pour the contents back into your mug.

NOTE: Always get a powdered chaga extract or brew your own chaga tea to reap all the benefits of this mushroom. Chaga mushrooms aren't edible, so traditionally it's been prepared as an extracted tea.

OATSTRAW INFUSION

SERVES 1

When you see the word *oats*, what image does your mind conjure? If a hot bowl of oatmeal comes to mind, you're not alone. While oats have a storied place in healthy diets around the world, in fact the entire plant boasts healing properties. Travel back in time and oatstraw—the straw of the oat plant—was used as an herbal remedy by folk healers in Europe and China, who prepared it as a tonic for the heart and nervous systems, and to treat insomnia.

Today research shows that oatstraw may indeed help improve mood by lowering stress, anxiety, and depression,[12] and it's shown promise in boosting brain functioning (in older adults), including memory and concentration,[13] and blood flow, especially to the heart.[14]

Some health food stores may carry dry oatstraw, or you can buy it online.

2 tablespoons dried oatstraw

1 tablespoon nettle leaves

1 tablespoon alfalfa leaves

1 tablespoon lemon balm leaves

1 tablespoon rose hips

Combine all the ingredients in a small mixing bowl.

Add 1 teaspoon of the mixture to a mug (you can also put the mixture into a tea ball, infuser, or teapot), and add 1 cup of hot water.

Steep for at least 6 minutes. Strain and enjoy.

NOTE: Store the oatstraw in an airtight jar and out of direct sunlight. Enjoy up to 2 times per day for best results.

HOLIDAY MULLED WINE

SERVES 6

Wine culture is so old that historians have found evidence of its consumption dating back thousands of years in ancient China, Greece, Lebanon, Egypt, and many other Old World countries. This versatile drink was (and still is) used for ceremonies, celebrations, and other religious rites—most likely because its complex flavors and symbology set it apart from other beverages, especially fermented ones.

This recipe, also known as *glühwein* or *glögg*, is an ancient European drink jammed with medicinal herbs that put the healing effects of wine over the top (while also cooking out some of the alcohol). The citrus is a digestive bitter, while the cardamom helps reduce inflammation.[15] The cinnamon acts as an aphrodisiac and relaxant,[16] the cloves are a natural painkiller that fight off bacterial and viral infections,[17] and star anise has been found to be just as effective against certain bacteria as antibiotics.[18] This recipe is easy to tweak to your preferences.

1 bottle full-bodied red wine (merlot, malbec, or cabernet sauvignon)

1 orange, sliced into rounds

1 lemon, sliced into rounds

1 small handful cinnamon sticks

4 to 6 whole cloves

1 to 2 star anise

2 to 3 cardamom pods

Optional sweetener: maple syrup or honey, to taste

Optional liqueur: brandy or spiced rum, to taste

Orange peel, for garnish

Extra cinnamon sticks, for garnish

....

Add all the ingredients to a large pot on the stove. Warm on the lowest setting for at least 1 hour.

Strain out the spices and fruit. Add the optional ingredients, if using.

Serve warm and garnished with an orange peel and a cinnamon stick.

NOTE: If you want to try this recipe without the alcohol, use half grape juice, half cranberry juice (low sugar is best) as a substitute.

FOUR-HERB BRAIN-BOOSTER TEA

SERVES 4

Want to boost your cognitive abilities? Then consider using ginkgo biloba. Native to Japan, Korea, and China, the ginkgo biloba is one of the oldest trees on earth. It's considered a "living fossil," existing for 270 million years without changing. In Traditional Chinese Medicine, ginkgo biloba has been used to treat circulation, asthma, vertigo, and fatigue, while in Iran it's been used to improve memory.[19] Recent studies show this unique tree can help increase energy and concentration by stimulating blood flow to your brain while simultaneously protecting it with powerful flavonoids.[20]

Ginkgo biloba has a mild flavor—although it's sometimes used as a digestive bitter—and it pairs well with other tasty brain-boosting herbs like lemon balm and tulsi.

1 tablespoon ginkgo biloba (you can find it in tea bags as well)

1 tablespoon dried lemon balm leaves

1 tablespoon dried holy basil (tulsi) leaves

1 slice fresh ginger

4 slices lemon

1 teaspoon honey, optional

In a medium saucepan, add all the herbs to 4 cups of water and bring to a simmer. Steep for at least 5 minutes. Strain and fill individual mugs.

Add 1 lemon slice per cup.

Wait for the water to cool down just a bit and then add the honey, if using. Serve immediately.

MAITAKE CHAI

Chai is a warm, spiced drink with ties to royalty and herbal medicine that dates back thousands of years. Legend has it that a king created this cleansing drink in order to promote Ayurvedic healing principles. While the word *chai* simply means "tea," the drink most people associate with chai is a black tea combined with warming spices, including ginger, cloves, and cinnamon, which aid in digestion and pain relief.

Instead of using black tea, we've added maitake mushrooms, a promising medicinal mushroom that has been used in traditional medicine for thousands of years. Maitake mushrooms are believed to support the immune system, boost energy, and improve concentration and brain functioning.

10 fresh or dried maitake strips

1 cinnamon stick

3 peppercorns

5 to 8 whole cloves

10 cardamom pods

A chunk of ginger

3 cups milk of your choice

Honey, optional

In a medium saucepan, simmer the maitake with 3 cups of water for 10 minutes.

Add the remaining herbs and simmer for another 10 minutes.

Strain and discard the ingredients, returning the tea to the saucepan.

Add milk and warm to your preference. Add the honey, if desired.

CHAGA LATTE ELIXIR

SERVES 1

Chaga has a storied history and was used in shamanic rituals, especially by the Khanty and Ostyak peoples. It was also used by the Ainu, the original inhabitants of Japan, for digestive upset and in religious ceremonies. Known as a "gift from God" by Siberian cultures, chaga is one of the most powerful medicinal mushrooms yet discovered. So much so that some people deem it the "king of the medicinal mushrooms."

Chaga contains high levels of antioxidants.[21] This alone makes it a powerhouse healer. Antioxidants are vital for fighting off free radicals, the very things that attack our healthy cells, making us sick. Thanks to its high antioxidant concentration, chaga has been shown to contain substances that may be beneficial in warding away many diseases, including certain cancers[22] and diabetes.[23]

Chaga is referred to as an immunomodulator, meaning it adapts to the needs of the immune system, similar to an adaptogenic herb.[24] This mighty mushroom can do this because it's rich in beta-glucans—a type of polysaccharide found in a variety of fungi. These compounds help balance the immune system by calming an overactive system or stimulating a slow one.

1 teaspoon chaga mushroom powder*

¼ teaspoon ground cinnamon

1 tablespoon coconut butter

½ teaspoon vanilla extract

¼ cup almond milk, warmed

Honey, to taste

A sprinkle of cinnamon or nutmeg, to serve (optional)

*If you're using chaga mushroom chunks, brew chaga tea per the brand's instructions in place of powder and hot water.

....

In a blender, combine all the ingredients with 1 cup of hot water and blend until smooth and frothy.

Pour into a mug and top with the extra sprinkle of cinnamon or nutmeg, if desired.

AYURVEDIC IMMUNE BOOSTER

SERVES 2

This tasty tea helps strengthen your immune system thanks to its adaptogenic properties, which help your body better manage stress.[25] Adaptogens and adaptogenic herbs are a pillar of the Ayurvedic healing traditions of ancient India. Adaptogenic plants like ashwagandha[26] and shatavari[27] have the remarkable ability to recalibrate your organ systems and restore balance. They "adapt" to whatever stressors (whether physical, chemical, or biological) are attacking your body and increase white blood cells when necessary to reduce your stress response.

Top that off with the antiviral, antibacterial, and anti-inflammatory healing properties of ginger,[28] cinnamon,[29] and honey,[30] and you have yourself a tea that will help you through the blistering cold and flu season, or any "feeling low" spells.

¼ tablespoon dried holy basil (tulsi)

¼ tablespoon ground ashwagandha root

¼ tablespoon ground shatavari root

½ tablespoon minced fresh ginger

2 cardamom pods

1 star anise

1 cinnamon stick

Honey, to taste

Milk, to taste

In a small saucepan, combine 2 cups of water with the holy basil, ashwagandha, shatavari, and ginger and heat on medium. Bring to a slight boil and then reduce the heat to low and simmer for 15 minutes.

Add the cardamom pods, star anise, and cinnamon and simmer for another 5 minutes.

Strain out the herbs.

Pour into two mugs, and allow to cool to lukewarm. To sweeten and cut some of the spice, add honey and milk to taste.

ASHWAGANDHA MILK

SERVES 1

Contributed by Tieraona Low Dog, M.D., internationally recognized expert and educator in the fields of integrative medicine, dietary supplements, herbal medicine, and women's health. Learn more at drlowdog.com.

Comfort in a cup. For thousands of years, the adaptogenic herb ashwagandha has been treasured in India for its ability to promote a healthy response to stress, create a sense of calm, and promote well-being. Traditionally, it's also been used to treat rheumatism, insomnia, joint pain and swelling, and nervous breakdowns. Recent studies have confirmed that ashwagandha is a natural stress reliever, and it may be beneficial in helping prevent and treat stress-related diseases and conditions such as arthritis, diabetes, and hypertension.[31]

It's traditionally prepared in milk, which I find the ideal base for this recipe. Many of us have so much on our plates that we have a hard time "turning off" our racing minds before bed. I find drinking a warm mug of ashwagandha milk in the evening is a wonderful way to unwind after a busy day.

12 ounces milk or nondairy alternative

½ to 1 teaspoon dried ashwagandha root, sliced

2 pitted dates, sliced

½ teaspoon ground cinnamon

....

Add all the ingredients to a saucepan and heat over low to medium heat. Bring to a boil. Turn down the heat, cover, and simmer for 10 minutes.

Strain and pour into a mug.

MORNING MACA ELIXIR

Used by indigenous people in Peru tracing back as far as 3800 B.C., maca has been cultivated for both its nutritional and medicinal value. Incan legend says that warriors depended upon maca for strength and ferocity in battle. Grown at altitudes of 7,000 to 11,000 feet, the radish-like maca contains significant amounts of amino acids, carbohydrates, B vitamins, and minerals, including calcium, phosphorus, zinc, magnesium, and iron.

Maca is also considered to be a fertility enhancer and aphrodisiac, partly due to the enhanced blood flow one experiences after ingesting it.[32] Known to "get things going" in the romance department, this sacred root was used during wedding rituals in ancient Andean culture. A hardy plant that can endure an extreme climate, full of health-giving properties, revered for thousands of years . . . now that's a sacred superfood.

1 to 2 cups unsweetened almond milk (enough to cover the other ingredients)

¼ cup raw hemp protein powder

2 tablespoons chia seeds or flaxseeds

1 teaspoon ground cinnamon

1 banana, or diced apple, pear, or mango

1½ tablespoons maca powder*

1 tablespoon wild honey (optional)

4 or 5 ice cubes

*You can find maca powder at health food stores or online.

....

Place all the ingredients in a blender. Blend until the elixir reaches the desired consistency.

NOTE: If you want to add a little extra oomph to your smoothie, try adding a pinch of cayenne pepper. This bold spice is extremely good for blood circulation.

GiNGER iNTENTiON TONiC

Recipe contributed by Mileen Patel, programming director, Sacred Science.

There is something sacred and spiritual that often arises when we drink tea with intention. A feeling of connectedness that has its own healing quality washes over us. In ancient Japan Buddhist monks created elaborate tea ceremonies partly designed to help participants experience more peace of mind and serenity. This recipe not only features healing herbs such as ginger, mint, and basil, which offer many health benefits like aiding digestion, but it also invites you into a place of connection, ritual, and intention—all elements that foster a healing environment for your entire being.

The idea is to add intention to the entire process, from the making of the tonic all the way through your ingestion of it. You do this by infusing thoughts—spoken aloud or silently—that focus on what you want the tonic to provide you with. For instance, more energy and vitality, peace, openness to love, surrendering to the unknown. (We offer more instruction on this in the recipe.) The bottom line: preparing and drinking this beverage is an invitation to turning the self-care of your mind, body, and spirit into a positive habit that feeds into a virtuous cycle.

There's a lot to play with in this recipe besides your intentions. You can use just the herbs, and/or use more or less of any ingredient to suit your taste. For those practicing Ayurveda, you can wait until it cools to room temperature to add in the honey.

1 tablespoon finely grated ginger (peel before grating)

¼ cup mint, basil, or chopped lemongrass (your choice)

1 to 2 pinches of finely ground Himalayan salt

2 to 3 teaspoons lime or lemon juice

2 to 3 teaspoons raw honey

. . . .

Heat 8 cups of water in a saucepan or pot until it's boiling.

While it's heating up, start thinking about what this tonic will be for you today.

Add the ginger and your choice of green herb.

Turn the heat down to a simmer (the greens may stay at the top, but the ginger should be moving around).

Simmer uncovered for about 15 minutes (you should have about 5 cups remaining).

While it's simmering, start another ritual or practice, such as meditating, exercising, going for a walk, breath work, squats, journaling, drawing, dancing, stretching . . . anything you enjoy.

Cut the heat and let it cool for 5 to 10 minutes, depending on how hot you like your tonic.

While it's cooling, continue your ritual or start a different, shorter one.

Add the salt, then the juice, and finally the honey.

Stir the tonic 10 times counterclockwise and then 10 times clockwise, until the honey is dissolved. Repeat if necessary.

(CONTINUED)

Put your hands over the container and look at the water, noticing your reflection.

Take a moment to think or say whatever you want to infuse the tonic with and subsequently ingest, such as hydration, detoxification, energy, nourishment, gratitude, abundance, or a good rest of your day. There's no right or wrong intention as it's personalized to you.

While continuing to look at the water and your reflection, think or say the words "thank you, I love you." It's hard not to smile when you do this.

Strain the tonic and enjoy it warm with the energy of your intention.

NOTE: You can also enjoy this drink chilled. Sprinkle in a little roasted ground cumin and you'll have Indian Lemonade with a little kick and a lot of intention.

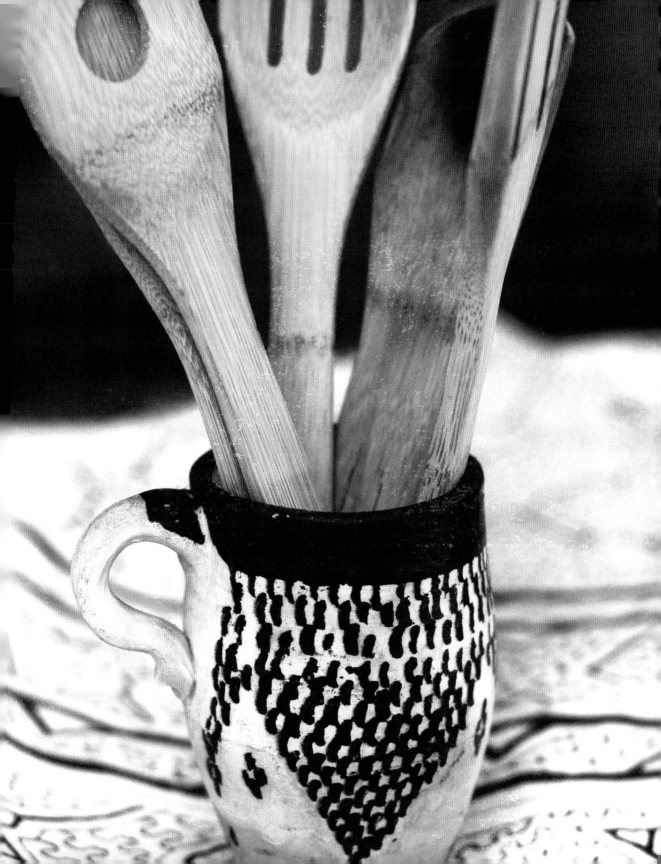

METRIC CONVERSION CHART

STANDARD CUP	FINE POWDER (E.G., FLOUR)	GRAIN (E.G., RICE)	GRANULAR (E.G., SUGAR)	LIQUID SOLIDS (E.G., BUTTER)	LIQUID (E.G., MILK)
1	140 g	150 g	190 g	200 g	240 ml
¾	105 g	113 g	143 g	150 g	180 ml
⅔	93 g	100 g	125 g	133 g	160 ml
½	70 g	75 g	95 g	100 g	120 ml
⅓	47 g	50 g	63 g	67 g	80 ml
¼	35 g	38 g	48 g	50 g	60 ml
⅛	18 g	19 g	24 g	25 g	30 ml

USEFUL EQUIVALENTS FOR LIQUID INGREDIENTS BY VOLUME				
¼ tsp			1 ml	
½ tsp			2 ml	
1 tsp			5 ml	
3 tsp	1 tbsp		½ fl oz	15 ml
	2 tbsp	⅛ cup	1 fl oz	30 ml
	4 tbsp	¼ cup	2 fl oz	60 ml
	5 ⅓ tbsp	⅓ cup	3 fl oz	80 ml
	8 tbsp	½ cup	4 fl oz	120 ml
	10 ⅔ tbsp	⅔ cup	5 fl oz	160 ml
	12 tbsp	¾ cup	6 fl oz	180 ml
	16 tbsp	1 cup	8 fl oz	240 ml
	1 pt	2 cups	16 fl oz	480 ml
	1 qt	4 cups	32 fl oz	960 ml
			33 fl oz	1000 ml 1L

USEFUL EQUIVALENTS FOR DRY INGREDIENTS BY WEIGHT

TO CONVERT OUNCES TO GRAMS, MULTIPLY THE NUMBER OF OUNCES BY 30.

1 oz	1/16 lb	30 g
4 oz	1/4 lb	120 g
8 oz	1/2 lb	240 g
12 oz	3/4 lb	360 g
16 oz	1 lb	480 g

USEFUL EQUIVALENTS FOR COOKING/OVEN TEMPERATURES

PROCESS	FAHRENHEIT	CELSIUS	GAS MARK
Freeze Water	32° F	0° C	
Room Temperature	68° F	20° C	
Boil Water	212° F	100° C	
Bake	325° F	160° C	3
	350° F	180° C	4
	375° F	190° C	5
	400° F	200° C	6
	425° F	220° C	7
	450° F	230° C	8
Broil			Grill

USEFUL EQUIVALENTS FOR LENGTH

TO CONVERT INCHES TO CENTIMETERS, MULTIPLY THE NUMBER OF INCHES BY 2.5.

1 in			2.5 cm	
6 in	1/2 ft		15 cm	
12 in	1 ft		30 cm	
36 in	3 ft	1 yd	90 cm	
40 in			100 cm	1 m

ENDNOTES

INTRODUCTION

1. Javier Rúa et al., "Combination of Carvacrol and Thymol: Antimicrobial Activity Against *Staphylococcus aureus* and Antioxidant Activity," *Foodborne Pathogens and Disease* 16, no. 9 (September 4, 2019): 622–29. http://doi .org/10.1089/fpd.2018.2594.
2. Min Lu et al., "Bactericidal Property of Oregano Oil Against Multidrug-Resistant Clinical Isolates," *Frontiers in Microbiology* 9 (October 5, 2018): 23–29. doi:10.3389 /fmicb.2018.02329.

LEAVES OF GRACE

1. T. S. Kahlon et al., "In Vitro Binding of Bile Acids by Spinach, Kale, Brussels Sprouts, Broccoli, Mustard Greens, Green Bell Pepper, Cabbage and Collards," *Food Chemistry* 100, no. 4 (2007): 1531–36. doi.org/10.1016 /j.foodchem.2005.12.020.
2. Ibid.
3. Bao Le et al., "Enhancement of the Anti-Inflammatory Effect of Mustard Kimchi on RAW 264.7 Macrophages by the *Lactobacillus plantarum* Fermentation-Mediated Generation of Phenolic Compound Derivatives," *Foods* 9, no. 2 (February 12, 2020): 181. doi:10.3390/foods9020181.
4. Youngeun Kwak et al., "Anti-Cancer Activities of Brassica juncea Leaves in Vitro," *EXCLI Journal* 15 (November 15, 2016): 699–710. doi:10.17179/excli2016-586.
5. Mehrnaz Nikkhah Bodagh et al., "Ginger in Gastrointestinal Disorders: A Systematic Review of Clinical Trials," *Food Science and Nutrition* 7, no. 1 (November 5, 2018): 96–108. doi:10.1002/fsn3.807.
6. Nafiseh Shokri Mashhadi et al., "Anti-Oxidative and Anti-Inflammatory Effects of Ginger in Health and Physical Activity: Review of Current Evidence," *International Journal of Preventive Medicine* 4, Suppl 1 (April 2013): S36–42. https://pubmed.ncbi.nlm.nih.gov /23717767/.
7. E. M. Bartels et al., "Efficacy and Safety of Ginger in Osteoarthritis Patients: A Meta-Analysis of Randomized Placebo-Controlled Trials," *Osteoarthritis and Cartilage* 23, no. 1 (January 2015): 13–21. https://doi.org/10.1016 /j.joca.2014.09.024.
8. Fang Cheng Wong et al., "The Anti-Cancer Activities of Vernonia amygdalina Extract in Human Breast Cancer Cell Lines Are Mediated Through Caspase-Dependent and P53-Independent Pathways," *PloS One* 8, no. 10 (October 24, 2013): e78021. doi:10.1371/journal.pone .0078021.
9. G. Murillo and R. G. Mehta, "Cruciferous Vegetables and Cancer Prevention," *Nutrition and Cancer* 41, nos. 1–2 (February 2001): 17-28. doi:10.1080/01635581.2001.968 0607.
10. Kahlon et al., 2007.
11. Shashank Kumar and Abhay K Pandey, "Chemistry and Biological Activities of Flavonoids: An Overview," *The Scientific World Journal* 2013 (December 29, 2013): 162750. doi:10.1155/2013/162750.
12. Alexander Yashin et al., "Antioxidant Activity of Spices and Their Impact on Human Health: A Review," *Antioxidants*, 6, no. 3 (September 15, 2017): 70. doi:10.3390/antiox6030070.
13. Bin Shan et al., "Antioxidant Capacity of 26 Spice Extracts and Characterization of Their Phenolic Constituents," *Journal of Agricultural and Food Chemistry* 53, no. 20 (October 5, 2005): 7749–59. doi:10.1021 /jf051513y.

MAJESTIC MUSHROOMS

1. Thomas Carlyle, *Sartor Resartus* (New York, NY: Oxford University Press, 2008).
2. María Elena Valverde et al., "Edible Mushrooms: Improving Human Health and Promoting Quality Life," *International Journal of Microbiology* 2015 (January 20, 2015): 376387. doi:10.1155/2015/376387.
3. Ibid.
4. Kristin Romey. "Here's What the Iceman Was Wearing When He Died 5,300 Years Ago," *National Geographic* 18 (August 2016). https://www.nationalgeographic.com

/culture/article/otzi-iceman-european-alps-mummy
-clothing-dna-leather-fur-archaeology.

5. Yongqi Tan et al., "Chemical Profiles and Health-
Promoting Effects of Porcini Mushroom (Boletus edulis):
A Narrative Review," *Food Chemistry* 390 (October 1,
2022): 133199. doi:10.1016/j.foodchem.2022.133199.

6. Davood Nasiry et al., "Anti-Inflammatory and Wound-
Healing Potential of Golden Chanterelle Mushroom,
Cantharellus cibarius (Agaricomycetes)," *International
Journal of Medicinal Mushrooms* 19, no. 10 (2017): 893–
903. doi:10.1615/IntJMedMushrooms.2017024674.

7. Zipora Tietel and Segula Masaphy, "True Morels
(Morchella)—Nutritional and Phytochemical
Composition, Health Benefits and Flavor: A Review,"
Critical Reviews in Food Science and Nutrition 58, no. 11
(July 24, 2018): 1888–1901. doi:10.1080/10408398.2017.1
285269.

8. Y. -R. Jin et al., "The Effect of Taraxacum officinale
on Gastric Emptying and Smooth Muscle Motility
in Rodents," *Neurogastroenterology and Motility: The
Official Journal of the European Gastrointestinal Motility
Society* 23, no. 8 (April 1, 2011): 766–e333. doi:10.1111
/j.1365-2982.2011.01704.

9. Xiaoshuang Dai et al., "Consuming Lentinula edodes
(Shiitake) Mushrooms Daily Improves Human Immunity:
A Randomized Dietary Intervention in Healthy Young
Adults," *Journal of the American College of Nutrition* 34, no.
6 (April 11, 2015): 478–87. doi:10.1080/07315724
.2014.950391.

10. Tongtong Xu et al., "The Cancer Preventive Effects of
Edible Mushrooms," *Anti-Cancer Agents in Medicinal
Chemistry* 12, no. 10 (December 2012): 1255–63.
doi:10.2174/187152012803833017.

11. Vaclav Vetvicka and Jana Vetvickova, "Immune-
Enhancing Effects of Maitake (Grifola frondosa)
and Shiitake (Lentinula edodes) Extracts," *Annals of
Translational Medicine* 2, no. 2 (February 2014): 14.
doi:10.3978/j.issn.2305-5839.2014.01.05.

12. Ibid.

13. K. M. Höld et al., "Alpha-Thujone (the Active Component
of Absinthe): Gamma-Aminobutyric Acid Type A
Receptor Modulation and Metabolic Detoxification,"
*Proceedings of the National Academy of Sciences of the United
States of America* 97, no. 8 (April 11, 2000): 3826–31.
doi:10.1073/pnas.070042397.

14. Ibid.

15. Christine Brock et al., "American Skullcap (Scutellaria
lateriflora): A Randomised, Double-Blind Placebo-
Controlled Crossover Study of Its Effects on Mood in
Healthy Volunteers," *Phytotherapy Research: PTR* 28, no. 5
(2014): 692–98. doi:10.1002/ptr.5044.

16. Chin-Chuan Tsai et al., "Using the Chinese Herb
Scutellaria barbata Against Extensively Drug-Resistant
Acinetobacter baumannii Infections: In Vitro and In Vivo
Studies," *BMC Complementary and Alternative Medicine* 18,
no. 1 (March 20, 2018): 96. doi:10.1186/s12906-018
-2151-7.

17. Elisa Tripoli et al., "The Phenolic Compounds of Olive
Oil: Structure, Biological Activity and Beneficial Effects
on Human Health," *Nutrition Research Reviews* 18, no. 1
(June 2005): 98–112. doi:10.1079/NRR200495.

18. Marta Guasch-Ferré, et al., "Olive Oil Consumption
and Cardiovascular Risk in U.S. Adults." *Journal of the
American College of Cardiology* 75, no. 15 (March 5, 2020):
1729–1739. doi:10.1016/j.jacc.2020.02.036.

19. Suthawan Charoenprasert and Alyson Mitchell, "Factors
Influencing Phenolic Compounds in Table Olives (Olea
europaea)," *Journal of Agricultural and Food Chemistry* 60,
no. 29 (July 25, 2012): 7081–95. doi:10.1021/jf3017699.

SOUPS AND STEWS FOR THE SOUL

1. Pasupuleti Visweswara Rao and Siew Hua Gan,
"Cinnamon: A Multifaceted Medicinal Plant," *Evidence-
Based Complementary and Alternative Medicine*, vol. 2014
(April 10, 2014): 642942. doi:10.1155/2014/642942.

2. S. Kirkham et al., "The Potential of Cinnamon to Reduce
Blood Glucose Levels in Patients with Type 2 Diabetes
and Insulin Resistance," *Diabetes, Obesity and Metabolism*
11, no. 12 (December 2009): 1100–13. doi:10.1111
/j.1463-1326.2009.01094.

3. Jayesh Sanmukhani et al., "Efficacy and Safety of
Curcumin in Major Depressive Disorder: A Randomized
Controlled Trial," *Phytotherapy Research: PTR*, 28, no. 4
(April 2014): 579–85. doi:10.1002/ptr.5025.

4. Mohammad Reza Khazdair et al., "The Effects of Crocus
sativus (saffron) and Its Constituents on Nervous System:
A Review." *Avicenna Journal of Phytomedicine* vol. 5, no. 5
(September–October 2015): 37691. https://www.ncbi.nlm.
nih.gov/pmc/articles/PMC4599112/.

5. Clare Gilbert, "What Is Vitamin A and Why Do We
Need It?" *Community Eye Health* 26, no. 84 (December
2013): 65. https://www.ncbi.nlm.nih.gov/pmc/articles
/PMC3936685/.

6. Susan Hewlings, "Coconuts and Health: Different
Chain Lengths of Saturated Fats Require Different
Consideration," *Journal of Cardiovascular Development and
Disease* 7, no. 4 (December 17, 2020): 59. doi:10.3390
/jcdd7040059.

7. Ibid.

8. Daniela Graf et al., "Cooked Red Lentils Dose-
Dependently Modulate the Colonic Microenvironment in
Healthy C57Bl/6 Male Mice," *Nutrients* 11, no. 8 (August
9, 2019): 1853. doi:10.3390/nu11081853.

9. Nobuhiro Kawai et al., "The Sleep-Promoting and Hypothermic Effects of Glycine Are Mediated by NMDA Receptors in the Suprachiasmatic Nucleus," *Neuropsychopharmacology: Official Publication of the American College of Neuropsychopharmacology* 40, no. 6 (May 2015): 1405–16. doi:10.1038/npp.2014.326.

10. Suqin Zhu et al. "Gelatin versus Its Two Major Degradation Products, Prolyl-Hydroxyproline and Glycine, As Supportive Therapy in Experimental Colitis in Mice," *Food Science & Nutrition* 6, no. 4 (April 16, 2018):1023–31. doi:10.1002/fsn3.639.

11. Najate Achamrah et al., "Glutamine and the Regulation of Intestinal Permeability: From Bench to Bedside," *Current Opinion in Clinical Nutrition and Metabolic Care* 20, no. 1 (January 2017): 86–91. doi:10.1097/MCO .0000000000000339.

12. Der-Jen Hsu et al., "Essential and Toxic Metals in Animal Bone Broths," *Food and Nutrition Research* 61, no. 1 (July 18, 2017): 1347478. doi:10.1080/16546628.2017 .1347478.

13. Petra Kavalcová et al., "Evaluation and Comparison of the Content of Total Polyphenols and Antioxidant Activity in Onion, Garlic and Leek," *Potravinarstvo* 8, no. 1. (November 2014). https://doi.org/10.5219/394.

14. Rafaela Ribeiro Silva et al., "Anti-Inflammatory, Antioxidant, and Antimicrobial Activities of Cocos nucifera Var. Typica," *BMC Complementary and Alternative Medicine* 13, no. 107 (May 16, 2013). doi:10.1186 /1472-6882-13-107.

15. Isao Kubo, et al., "Antibacterial Activity of Coriander Volatile Compounds Against Salmonella choleraesuis," *Journal of Agricultural and Food Chemistry* 52, no. 11 (June 2, 2004): 3329–32. doi:10.1021/jf0354186.

TINY WONDERS

1. Morrisa Engles, "Cacao in Olmec Society," Boston University (July 20, 2017). https://sites.bu.edu /gastronomyblog/2017/07/20/cacao-in-olmec-society/.

2. Tasleem A. Zafar and Yearul Kabir, "Chickpeas Suppress Postprandial Blood Glucose Concentration, and Appetite and Reduce Energy Intake at the Next Meal," *Journal of Food Science and Technology* 54, no. 4 (March 2017): 987–94. doi:10.1007/s13197-016-2422-6.

3. Juárez-Chairez Milagros Faridy et al., "Biological Activities of Chickpea in Human Health (Cicer arietinum L.). A Review," *Plant Foods for Human Nutrition* 75, no. 2 (June 2020): 142–53. doi:10.1007/s11130-020-00814-2.

4. Anna E. Kirkland et al., "The Role of Magnesium in Neurological Disorders," *Nutrients* 10, no. 6 (June 6, 2018): 730. doi:10.3390/nu10060730.

5. Jessica Wang et al., "Zinc, Magnesium, Selenium and Depression: A Review of the Evidence, Potential Mechanisms and Implications," *Nutrients* 10, no. 5 (May 9, 2018): 584. doi:10.3390/nu10050584.

6. Faiqa Zulfqar et al., "Chemical Characterization, Antioxidant Evaluation, and Antidiabetic Potential of Pinus Gerardiana (Pine Nuts) Extracts," *Journal of Food Biochemistry* 44, no. 6 (June 2020): e13199. doi:10.1111 /jfbc.13199.

7. Jackson A. Seukep et al., "Antibacterial Activities of the Methanol Extracts of Seven Cameroonian Dietary Plants Against Bacteria Expressing MDR Phenotypes," *SpringerPlus* 2, no. 363 (July 31, 2013). springerplus. springeropen.com/articles/10.1186/2193-1801-2-363.

8. Erika Maria Henriques Monteiro et al., "Antinociceptive and Anti-Inflammatory Activities of the Sesame Oil and Sesamin," *Nutrients* 6, no. 5 (May 12, 2014): 1931–44. doi:10.3390/nu6051931.

BURIED TREASURES

1. Mycaela Crouse, "Inca Medicine: Religion, Culture, and Ethnobotany," Central College, Pella, IA (2015). central. edu/writing-anthology/2019/05/29/inca-medicine-religion-culture-and-ethnobotany/.

2. A. Jajja et al., "Beetroot Supplementation Lowers Daily Systolic Blood Pressure in Older, Overweight Subjects," *Nutrition Research* 34, no. 10 (October 2014): 868–75. doi:10.1016/j.nutres.2014.09.007.

3. Qi-Jun Wu et al., "Cruciferous Vegetable Consumption and Gastric Cancer Risk: A Meta-Analysis of Epidemiological Studies," *Cancer Science* 104, no. 8 (August 2013): 1067–73. doi:10.1111/cas.12195.

GODLY GRAINS

1. Musthafa Mohamed Essa et al., "Beneficial Effects of Date Palm Fruits on Neurodegenerative Diseases," *Neural Regeneration Research* 11, no. 7 (July 2016): 1071–72. https://doi:10.4103/1673-5374.187032.

2. Lin Nie et al., "Avenanthramide, A Polyphenol from Oats, Inhibits Vascular Smooth Muscle Cell Proliferation and Enhances Nitric Oxide Production," *Atherosclerosis* 186, no. 2 (June 2006): 260–66. doi:10.1016/j.atherosclerosis .2005.07.027.

3. Khawaja Muhammad Imran Bashir and Jae-Suk Choi, "Clinical and Physiological Perspectives of β-Glucans: The Past, Present, and Future," *International Journal of Molecular Sciences* 18, no. 9 (September 5, 2017): 1906. 5doi:10.3390/ijms18091906.

4. Jørgen Valeur et al., "Oatmeal Porridge: Impact on Microflora-Associated Characteristics in Healthy Subjects," *The British Journal of Nutrition* 115, no. 1 (January 14, 2016): 62–67. https://doi:10.1017 /S0007114515004213.

5. Candida J. Rebello et al., "Dietary Fiber and Satiety: The Effects of Oats on Satiety," *Nutrition Reviews* 74, no. 2 (February 2016): 131–47. doi:10.1093/nutrit/nuv063.

6. Sheng Siyuan et al., "Corn Phytochemicals and Their Health Benefits," *Food Science and Human Wellness* 7, no. 3 (September 2018): 185–195. https://doi.org/10.1016/j.fshw.2018.09.003.

7. Kaye Foster-Powell et al., "International Table of Glycemic Index and Glycemic Load Values: 2002," *The American Journal of Clinical Nutrition* 76, no. 1 (July 2002): 5–56. doi:10.1093/ajcn/76.1.5.

8. Emily T. Nuss and Sherry A. Tanumihardjo, "Maize: A Paramount Staple Crop in the Context of Global Nutrition," *Comprehensive Reviews in Food Science and Food Safety* 9, no. 4 (July 2010): 417–36. doi.org/10.1111/j.1541-4337.2010.00117.x.

9. Matsuda Sanae and Aoyagi Yasuo, "Green Asparagus (Asparagus officinalis) Prevented Hypertension by an Inhibitory Effect on Angiotensin-Converting Enzyme Activity in the Kidney of Spontaneously Hypertensive Rats," *Journal of Agricultural and Food Chemistry* 61, no. 23 (June 12, 2013): 5520–25. doi:10.1021/jf3041066.

10. Deb Mandal Manisha and Shyamapada Mandal, "Honey: Its Medicinal Property and Antibacterial Activity," *Asian Pacific Journal of Tropical Biomedicine* 1, no. 2 (April 2011): 154–60. doi:10.1016/S2221-1691(11)60016-6.

MASTERS OF WATER AND AIR

1. Luc Djoussé et al., "Fish Consumption, Omega-3 Fatty Acids and Risk of Heart Failure: A Meta-Analysis," *Clinical Nutrition* 31, no. 6 (December 2012): 846–53. doi:10.1016/j.clnu.2012.05.010.

2. Martha Clare Morris et al., "Fish Consumption and Cognitive Decline with Age in a Large Community Study," *Archives of Neurology* 62, no. 12 (December 2005): 1849–53. doi:10.1001/archneur.62.12.noc50161.

3. Giuseppe Grosso et al., "Omega-3 Fatty Acids and Depression: Scientific Evidence and Biological Mechanisms," *Oxidative Medicine and Cellular Longevity* 2014 (March 2014): 313570. doi:10.1155/2014/313570.

4. Dalal Hammoudi Halat et al., "A Focused Insight into Thyme: Biological, Chemical, and Therapeutic Properties of an Indigenous Mediterranean Herb," *Nutrients* 14, no. 10 (May 18, 2022): 2104. doi:10.3390/nu14102104.

5. V. Lagouri and D. Boskou, "Nutrient Antioxidants in Oregano," *International Journal of Food Sciences and Nutrition* 47, no. 6 (November 1996): 493–97. doi:10.3109/09637489609031878.

6. Sabahat Saeed and Perween Tariq, "Antibacterial Activity of Oregano (Origanum vulgare Linn.) Against Gram Positive Bacteria," *Pakistan Journal of Pharmaceutical Sciences* 22, no. 4 (October 2009): 421–24. https://pubmed.ncbi.nlm.nih.gov/19783523/.

7. D. H. Gilling et al., "Antiviral Efficacy and Mechanisms of Action of Oregano Essential Oil and Its Primary Component Carvacrol Against Murine Norovirus," *Journal of Applied Microbiology* 116, no. 5 (February 12, 2014): 1149–63. doi:10.1111/jam.12453.

8. Bart Pennings et al., "Minced Beef Is More Rapidly Digested and Absorbed Than Beef Steak, Resulting in Greater Postprandial Protein Retention in Older Men," *The American Journal of Clinical Nutrition* 98, no. 1 (July 2013): 121–28. doi:10.3945/ajcn.112.051201.

9. M. Alamgeer, et al., "Pharmacological Evaluation of Antihypertensive Effect of Aerial Parts of Thymus Linearis Benth," *Acta Poloniae Pharmaceutica* 71, no. 4 (July –August 2014): 677–82. https://pubmed.ncbi.nlm.nih.gov/25272894/.

10. Margherita Zotti et al., "Carvacrol: From Ancient Flavoring to Neuromodulatory Agent," *Molecules* 18, no. 6 (May 24, 2013): 6161–72. doi:10.3390/molecules18066161.

11. Dominik Szwajgier et al., "The Neuroprotective Effects of Phenolic Acids: Molecular Mechanism of Action," *Nutrients* 9, no. 5 (May 10, 2017): 477. doi:10.3390/nu9050477.

12. J. M. Hills and P. I. Aaronson, "The Mechanism of Action of Peppermint Oil on Gastrointestinal Smooth Muscle. An Analysis Using Patch Clamp Electrophysiology and Isolated Tissue Pharmacology in Rabbit and Guinea Pig," *Gastroenterology* 101, no. 1 (July 1991): 55–65. doi:10.1016/0016-5085(91)90459-x.

DRIED AND CURED WITH CARE

1. Alvaro Montoya-Rodríguez et al., "Extrusion Improved the Anti-Inflammatory Effect of Amaranth (Amaranthus hypochondriacus) Hydrolysates in LPS-Induced Human THP-1 Macrophage-Like and Mouse RAW 264.7 Macrophages by Preventing Activation of NF-Kb Signaling," *Molecular Nutrition and Food Research* 58, no. 5 (January 15, 2014): 1028–41. doi:10.1002/mnfr.201300764.

2. Mariann Garner-Wizard et al., "Chia (Salvia hispanica) and Its Long History of Use Reveals Future Potential," American Botanical Council, issue 269, (November 2004). https://www.herbalgram.org/resources/herbclip/issues/bin_269/review44017/.

3. Rahman Ullah et al., "Nutritional and Therapeutic Perspectives of Chia (Salvia hispanica L.): A Review," *Journal of Food Science and Technology* 53, no. 4 (April 2016): 1750–58. doi:10.1007/s13197-015-1967-0.

4. Ibid.

5. Mihir Parikh et al., "Dietary Flaxseed as a Strategy for Improving Human Health," *Nutrients* 11, no. 5 (May 25, 2019): 1171. doi:10.3390/nu11051171.

6. Karin Ried et al., "Effect of Cocoa on Blood Pressure," *The Cochrane Database of Systematic Reviews* 4, no. 4 (April 25, 2017): CD008893. doi:10.1002/14651858.CD008893.pub3.

7. Farzeneh Sorond et al., "Cerebral Blood Flow Response to Flavanol-Rich Cocoa in Healthy Elderly Humans," *Neuropsychiatric Disease and Treatment* 4, no. 2 (April 2008): 433–40. ncbi.nlm.nih.gov/pmc/articles/PMC2518374/.

8. Alexander N. Sokolov et al., "Chocolate and the Brain: Neurobiological Impact of Cocoa Flavanols on Cognition and Behavior," *Neuroscience and Biobehavioral Reviews* 37, no. 10 Pt 2 (December 2013): 2445–53. doi:10.1016/j.neubiorev.2013.06.013.

9. Arshad H. Rahmani et al., "Therapeutic Effects of Date Fruits (Phoenix dactylifera) in the Prevention of Diseases via Modulation of Anti-Inflammatory, Anti-Oxidant and Anti-Tumour Activity," *International Journal of Clinical and Experimental Medicine* 7, no. 3 (March 15, 2014): 483–91. https://www.ncbi.nlm.nih.gov/pmc/articles/PMC3992385/.

10. Charlotte Bamberger et al., "A Walnut-Enriched Diet Affects Gut Microbiome in Healthy Caucasian Subjects: A Randomized, Controlled Trial," *Nutrients* 10, no. 2 (February 22, 2018): 244. doi:10.3390/nu10020244.

11. Shibu M. Poulose et al., "Role of Walnuts in Maintaining Brain Health with Age," *The Journal of Nutrition* 144, no. 4 Supplement (April 2014): 561S–566S. doi:10.3945/jn.113.184838.

BITTER, BRINY, AND BOLD

1. Z. Lu et al., "Bacteriophage Ecology in Commercial Sauerkraut Fermentations," *Applied and Environmental Microbiology* 69, no. 6 (June 2003): 3192–202. doi:10.1128/AEM.69.6.3192-3202.2003.

2. Manas Ranjan Swain et al., "Fermented Fruits and Vegetables of Asia: A Potential Source of Probiotics," *Biotechnology Research International* 2014 (May 28, 2014): 250424. doi:10.1155/2014/250424.

3. Seo-Jin Yang et al., "Antioxidant and Immune-Enhancing Effects of Probiotic Lactobacillus plantarum 200655 Isolated from Kimchi," *Food Science and Biotechnology* 28, no. 2 (September 27, 2018): 491–99. doi:10.1007/s10068-018-0473-3.

4. F. C. Ribeiro et al., "Action Mechanisms of Probiotics on Candida Spp. and Candidiasis Prevention: An Update," *Journal of Applied Microbiology* 129, no. 2 (August 2020): 175–85. doi:10.1111/jam.14511.

5. Minji Woo et al., "Bioactive Compounds in Kimchi Improve the Cognitive and Memory Functions Impaired by Amyloid Beta," *Nutrients* 10, no. 10 (October 20, 2018): 1554. doi:10.3390/nu10101554.

6. Peter Bucheli et al., "Biomolecular and Clinical Aspects of Chinese Wolfberry," in Iris F. F. Benzie and Sissi Wachtel-Galor, eds., *Herbal Medicine: Biomolecular and Clinical Aspects*, 2nd edition, (Boca Raton, FL: CRC Press/Taylor & Francis; 2011). ncbi.nlm.nih.gov/books/NBK92756/.

7. W. M. A. D. B. Fernando et al., "The Role of Dietary Coconut for the Prevention and Treatment of Alzheimer's Disease: Potential Mechanisms of Action," *British Journal of Nutrition* 114, no. 1 (July 14, 2015): 1–14. https://doi.org/10.1017/S0007114515001452.

8. Jan Borlinghaus et al., "Allicin: Chemistry and Biological Properties," *Molecules* 19, no. 8 (August 19, 2014) 12591–618. doi:10.3390/molecules190812591.

ENCHANTING SPICES AND SAUCES

1. K. P. Kochhar et al., "Gastro-Intestinal Effects of Indian Spice Mixture (Garam Masala)," *Tropical Gastroenterology: Official Journal of the Digestive Diseases Foundation* 20, no. 4 (October–December 1999): 170–4. pubmed.ncbi.nlm.nih.gov/10769605/.

2. S. Ankri and D. Mirelman, "Antimicrobial Properties of Allicin from Garlic," *Microbes and Infection* 1, no. 2 (February 1999): 125–29. doi:10.1016/s1286-4579(99)80003-3.

3. Johura Ansary et al., "Potential Health Benefit of Garlic Based on Human Intervention Studies: A Brief Overview," *Antioxidants* (Basel, Switzerland) 9, no. 7 (July 15, 2020): 619. doi:10.3390/antiox9070619.

4. Heeok Hong et al., "Effects of Pumpkin Seed Oil and Saw Palmetto Oil in Korean Men with Symptomatic Benign Prostatic Hyperplasia," *Nutrition Research and Practice* 3, no. 4 (Winter 2009): 323–27. doi:10.4162/nrp.2009.3.4.323.

5. H. O. Dickinson et al., "Magnesium Supplementation for the Management of Essential Hypertension in Adults," *The Cochrane Database of Systematic Reviews* 3, no. 3 (July 19, 2006): CD004640. doi:10.1002/14651858.CD004640.pub2/.

6. James M. Peacock et al., "Serum Magnesium and Risk of Sudden Cardiac Death in the Atherosclerosis Risk in Communities (ARIC) Study," *American Heart Journal* 160, no. 3 (September 2010): 464–70. doi:10.1016/j.ahj.2010.06.012.

7. Robert K. Rude et al., "Skeletal and Hormonal Effects of Magnesium Deficiency," *Journal of the American College of Nutrition* 28, no. 2 (April 2009): 131–41. doi:10.1080/07315724.2009.10719764.

8. Farideh Shishehbor et al., "Vinegar Consumption Can Attenuate Postprandial Glucose and Insulin Responses; a Systematic Review and Meta-Analysis of Clinical Trials," *Diabetes Research and Clinical Practice* 127 (May 2017): 1–9, https://doi.org/10.1016/j.diabres.2017.01.021.

9. Solaleh Sadat Khezri et al., "Beneficial Effects of Apple Cider Vinegar on Weight Management, Visceral Adiposity Index and Lipid Profile in Overweight or Obese Subjects Receiving Restricted Calorie Diet: A Randomized Clinical Trial," *Journal of Functional Foods* 43, (April 2018): 95–102. https://doi.org/10.1016/j.jff.2018.02.003.

10. Ibid.

11. Ana Carolina Loureiro Gama Mota et al., "Antifungal Activity of Apple Cider Vinegar on Candida Species Involved in Denture Stomatitis," *Journal of Prosthodontics* 24, no. 4, (June 2015): 296–302. doi.org/10.1111/jopr.12207.

12. Darsna Yagnik et al., "Antibacterial Apple Cider Vinegar Eradicates Methicillin Resistant *Staphylococcus aureus* and Resistant *Escherichia coli*," *Scientific Reports* 11 (January 2021): 1854. https://doi.org/10.1038/s41598-020-78407-x.

13. Shukranul Mawa et al., "Ficus carica L. (Moraceae): Phytochemistry, Traditional Uses and Biological Activities," *Evidence-Based Complementary and Alternative Medicine* 2013 (September 6, 2013): 974256. doi:10.1155/2013/974256.

TIME-TESTED TEAS AND TONICS

1. Hung-Sen Chen et al., "Studies on the Immuno-Modulating and Anti-Tumor Activities of Ganoderma lucidum (Reishi) Polysaccharides," *Bioorganic and Medicinal Chemistry* 12, no. 21 (November 2004): 5595–601. https://doi:10.1016/j.bmc.2004.08.003.

2. Djanggan Sargowo et al., "PS 02-02 Effect Ganoderma lucidum Polysaccharide Peptides as Anti-hypertension, Anti-lipid, Anti-oxidant, Anti-inflammation in High Risk Patients of Atherosclerosis," *Journal of Hypertension* 34 (September 2016): e105. doi: 10.1097/01.hjh.0000500132.15515.a3.

3. Sissi Wachtel-Galor et al, *Herbal Medicine: Biomolecular and Clinical Aspects*, (2nd edition), (Boca Raton: FL CRC Press/Taylor & Francis, 2011).

4. Marc Maurice Cohen, "Tulsi–Ocimum sanctum: A Herb for all Reasons," *Journal of Ayurveda and Integrative Medicine* 5, no. 4 (October–December 2014): 251–59. doi:10.4103/0975-9476.146554.

5. Emilija Ivanova Stojcheva and José Carlos Quintela, "The Effectiveness of *Rhodiola rosea* L. Preparations in Alleviating Various Aspects of Life-Stress Symptoms and Stress-Induced Conditions-Encouraging Clinical Evidence," *Molecules* 27, no. 12 (June 17, 2022): 3902. doi:10.3390/molecules27123902.

6. Shi-Bing Liang et al., "The Potential Effects and Use of Chinese Herbal Medicine Pine Pollen (*Pinus pollen*): A Bibliometric Analysis of Pharmacological and Clinical Studies," *World Journal of Traditional Chinese Medicine* 6, no. 2 (March 31, 2020): 163–70. doi:10.4103/wjtcm.wjtcm_4_20.

7. Giovambattista Desideri et al., "Benefits in Cognitive Function, Blood Pressure, and Insulin Resistance Through Cocoa Flavanol Consumption in Elderly Subjects with Mild Cognitive Impairment: The Cocoa, Cognition, and Aging (Cocoa) Study," *Hypertension* 60, no. 3 (August 14, 2012): 794–801. doi:10.1161/HYPERTENSIONAHA.112.193060.

8. Alexander N. Sokolov et al., "Chocolate and the Brain: Neurobiological Impact of Cocoa Flavanols on Cognition and Behavior," *Neuroscience and Biobehavioral Reviews* 37, no. 10 Pt 2 (December 2013): 2445–53. doi:10.1016/j.neubiorev.2013.06.013.

9. Quintino Reis De Araujo et al., "Cocoa and Human Health: From Head to Foot—A Review," *Critical Reviews in Food Science and Nutrition* 56, no. 1 (January 2, 2016): 1–12. doi:10.1080/10408398.2012.657921.

10. E. S. Mitchell et al., "Differential Contributions of Theobromine and Caffeine on Mood, Psychomotor Performance and Blood Pressure," *Physiology and Behavior* 104, no. 5 (October 24, 2011): 816–22. doi:10.1016/j.physbeh.2011.07.027.

11. S. K. Swanston-Flatt et al., "Glycaemic Effects of Traditional European Plant Treatments for Diabetes. Studies in Normal and Streptozotocin Diabetic Mice," *Diabetes Research* 10, no. 2 (February 1989): 69–73. ncbi.nlm.nih.gov/2743711/.

12. Vasantmeghna S. Murthy and Ajish G. Mangot, "Psychiatric Aspects of Phosphodiesterases: An Overview," *Indian Journal of Pharmacology* 47, no. 6 (November–December 2015): 594–99. doi:10.4103/0253-7613.169593.

13. Narelle M. Berry et al., "Acute Effects of an Avena Sativa Herb Extract on Responses to the Stroop Color-Word Test," *Journal of Alternative and Complementary Medicine* 17, no. 7 (July 2011): 635–37. doi:10.1089/acm.2010.0450.

14. Rachel H. X. Wong et al., "Chronic Consumption of a Wild Green Oat Extract (Neuravena) Improves Brachial Flow-Mediated Dilatation and Cerebrovascular Responsiveness in Older Adults," *Journal of Hypertension* 31, no. 1 (January 2013): 192–200. doi:10.1097/HJH.0b013e32835b04d4.

15. Md. Mizanur Rahman et al., "Cardamom Powder Supplementation Prevents Obesity, Improves Glucose

Intolerance, Inflammation and Oxidative Stress in Liver of High Carbohydrate High Fat Diet Induced Obese Rats," *Lipids in Health and Disease* 16, no. 1 (August 14, 2017): 151. doi:10.1186/s12944-017-0539-x.

16. Sumanta Kumar Goswami et al., "Efficacy of Cinnamomum cassia Blume. in Age Induced Sexual Dysfunction of Rats," *Journal of Young Pharmacists* 5, no. 4 (December 2013): 148–53. doi:10.1016/j.jyp.2013.11.001.

17. B. C. Nzeako et al., "Antimicrobial Activities of Clove and Thyme Extracts," *Sultan Qaboos University Medical Journal* 6, no. 1 (June 2006): 33–39. ncbi.nlm.nih.gov /pmc/articles/PMC3074903/.

18. Jyh-Ferng Yang et al., "Chemical Composition and Antibacterial Activities of Illicium Verum Against Antibiotic-Resistant Pathogens," *Journal of Medicinal Food* 13, no. 5 (October 2010): 1254–62. doi:10.1089 /jmf.2010.1086.

19. Zhi-Kun Sun et al., "Traditional Chinese Medicine: A Promising Candidate for the Treatment of Alzheimer's Disease," *Translational Neurodegeneration* 2, no. 1 (February 28, 2013): 6. doi:10.1186/2047-9158-2-6.

20. Tasiu Isah, "Rethinking Ginkgo biloba L.: Medicinal Uses and Conservation," *Pharmacognosy Reviews* 9, no. 18 (February 2015): 140–148. doi:10.4103/0973-7847.162137.

21. Yoo Kyoung Park et al., "Chaga Mushroom Extract Inhibits Oxidative DNA Damage in Human Lymphocytes as Assessed by Comet Assay," *BioFactors* 21, nos. 1–4 (2004): 109–12. doi:10.1002/biof.552210120.

22. Satoru Arata et al., "Continuous Intake of the Chaga Mushroom (Inonotus obliquus) Aqueous Extract Suppresses Cancer Progression and Maintains Body Temperature in Mice," *Heliyon* 2, no. 5 (May 12, 2016): e00111. doi:10.1016/j.heliyon.2016.e00111.

23. Yangpeng Lu et al., "Recent Developments in *Inonotus obliquus* (Chaga mushroom) Polysaccharides: Isolation, Structural Characteristics, Biological Activities and Application," *Polymers* 13, no. 9 (April 28, 2021): 1441. doi:10.3390/polym13091441.

24. Yeon-Ran Kim, "Immunomodulatory Activity of the Water Extract from Medicinal Mushroom Inonotus obliquus," *Mycobiology* 33, no. 3 (September 2005): 158–62. doi:10.4489/MYCO.2005.33.3.158.

25. Lian-Ying Liao et al., "A Preliminary Review of Studies on Adaptogens: Comparison of Their Bioactivity in TCM with That of Ginseng-Like Herbs Used Worldwide," *Chinese Medicine* 13, no. 1 (November 16, 2018): 57. doi:10.1186/s13020-018-0214-9.

26. Jeremy Mikolai et al., "In Vivo Effects of Ashwagandha (Withania somnifera) Extract on the Activation of Lymphocytes," *Journal of Alternative and Complementary Medicine* 15, no. 4 (April 2009): 423–30. doi:10.1089 /acm.2008.0215.

27. Manish Gautam et al., "Immunomodulatory Activity of Asparagus racemosus on Systemic Th1/Th2 Immunity: Implications for Immunoadjuvant Potential," *Journal of Ethnopharmacology* 121, no. 2 (January 21, 2009): 241–47. doi:10.1016/j.jep.2008.10.028.

28. M. Tauseef Sultan et al., "Immunity: Plants As Effective Mediators," *Critical Reviews in Food Science and Nutrition* 54, no.10 (February 24, 2014): 1298–308. doi:10.1080/104 08398.2011.633249.

29. Anne Schink et al., "Anti-Inflammatory Effects of Cinnamon Extract and Identification of Active Compounds Influencing the TLR2 and TLR4 Signaling Pathways," *Food and Function* 9, no. 11 (November 14, 2018): 5950–64. doi:10.1039/c8fo01286e.

30. Manisha Deb Mandal and Shyamapada Mandal, "Honey: Its Medicinal Property and Antibacterial Activity," *Asian Pacific Journal of Tropical Biomedicine* 1, no. 2 (April 2011): 154–60. doi:10.1016/S2221-1691(11)60016-6.

31. Narendra Singh et al., "An Overview on Ashwagandha: A Rasayana (Rejuvenator) of Ayurveda," *African Journal of Traditional, Complementary, and Alternative Medicines* 8, no. 5 (July 3, 2011): 208–13. doi:10.4314/ajtcam.v8i5S.9.

32. Gustavo F. Gonzales, "Ethnobiology and Ethnopharmacology of Lepidium meyenii (Maca), a Plant from the Peruvian Highlands," *Evidence-Based Complementary and Alternative Medicine* 2012 (October 2, 2012): 193496. doi:10.1155/2012/193496.

INDEX

A

adaptogens, 245, 246
Al Kabsa, 132–34
Ancient Herb-Marinated Chicken, 145
antiviral properties. *See colds and flu, fighting; viruses, fighting*
apple cider vinegar
    Honey Dijon Dressing, 212–13
    Shamanic Fire Cider, 187
Arabian Hummus, 90–91
arthritis, 18, 246
Ashwagandha Milk, 246–47
asparagus
    about: benefits and historical perspective, 118
    Asparagus Risotto, 118–19
Ayurveda
    Ayurvedic Immune Booster, 245
    chai and, 241
    fennel and, 211
    garam masala and, 30, 195
    holy basil as *Rasayana, 223*
    khichdi/kitchari and, 85
    lotus root and, 101
Aztec Granola Bars, 158–59

B

bacteria, fighting, 39, 47, 51, 58, 62, 90, 141, 187, 199, 212, 237, 245
bacteria, good, supporting gut, 65, 66, 97, 111, 122, 169, 172, 181, 184, 187, 199, 212
beans. *See legumes, seeds, and nuts*

beef
    about: hamburgers as medicinal, 142
    Nigerian Bitter Leaf Stew (Ofe Onugbu), 20–21
    Nourishing Protein Patties, 142–43
beets
    about: benefits and historical perspective, 94
    Roasted Winter Roots, 97
    Summer Borscht, 94–95
"before-meal" prayer, 10–11
Berbere Spice, 192–93
Berbers, about, 61
berries, in Timeless Trail Mix, 169
beverages. *See teas and tonics*
bison, in Cree Pemmican, 156–57
bitter leaf
    about: benefits and historical perspective, 20
    Nigerian Bitter Leaf Stew (Ofe Onugbu), 20–21
Black Fig Jam (Moraba 'Yeh Anjir), 216–17
blessing your food, 10–11
blood
    cleansing/improving, 20, 47, 48, 118, 199
    flow, improving, 149, 165, 234, 238, 249
blood pressure, lowering, 27, 56, 94, 111, 118, 145, 165, 187, 199, 202, 212, 220, 230
blood sugar levels, regulating, 56, 81, 82, 111, 115, 158, 229, 233
bone broth, 66–67
brain-booster tea, 238–39
breads and crackers

about: fermentation and sourdough, 122; making sourdough starter, 125; manna bread and Dead Sea Scrolls, 126
    Bean, Seed, and Herb Crackers, 162–63
    Choctaw Cornbread, 121
    Essene Sprouted Wheat Manna Bread, 126–27
    Ethiopian Injera, 183
    Sourdough Bread, 122–25
broccoli, in Mediterranean Kale Salad, 27

C

cabbage
    about: fermenting, 172; nutritional benefits, 172
    Korean Kimchi, 175–77
    Medicinal Chinese Dumplings, 149–53
    Mediterranean Kale Salad, 27
    Sacred Sauerkraut, 172–74
cacao and chocolate
    about: benefits and historical perspective, 165
    Cacao Bites, 165
    Mayan Hot Chocolate, 230–31
    Timeless Trail Mix, 169
calcium, 14, 27, 65, 66, 78, 89, 102, 158, 166, 180, 229, 249
cancer
    preventing, reducing risk, 43, 47, 52, 97, 98, 165, 199, 216, 242
    treating, fending off, 14, 17, 27, 39, 192

Caribbean Pepperpot Recipe, 73
Carlyle, Thomas, 36
carrots
      Roasted Winter Roots, 97
      salads with, 14, 27
cassareep, about, 73
cauliflower
      about: benefits and historical
            perspective, 28
      Roasted Cauliflower Steaks,
            28–29
Celtic Druids Honey Mead, 188–89
Chaga Latte Elixir, 242–43
chai, maitake, 241
cheese, in Saag Paneer, 30–31
chicken
      about: nutritional benefits, 132,
            145
      Al Kabsa, 132–34
      Ancient Herb-Marinated Chicken,
            145
      Caribbean Pepperpot Recipe, 73
      Fire-Roasted Chicken with Maya
            Adobo Sauce, 135–37
      Herbed Sausage, 146–47
      Nourishing Protein Patties,
            142–43
      Traditional Māori Puha Boil Up,
            70–71
chickpeas. See legumes, seeds,
      and nuts
chicory
      about: benefits and historical
            perspective, 24
      Summer Chicory Salad, 24–25
Chimichurri, 207
Chinese dumplings. See Medicinal
      Chinese Dumplings
Chinese medicine. See Traditional
      Chinese Medicine
chocolate. See cacao and chocolate
Choctaw Cornbread, 121
cholesterol, lowering, 17, 27, 111,
      187, 199, 212
cinnamon, about, 56
citrus
      about: cooking fish without heat
            using, 138
      Lemon Quinoa Salad with Hemp
            Seed, 89
      Lemon-Garlic Dressing, 27

coconut milk
      about, 74
      Homemade Coconut Milk,
            224–25
coffee alternative, herbal, 233
cold sores, healing, 172
colds and flu, fighting, 74, 81, 187,
      212, 225, 245
collard greens, in Greens in
      Groundnut Sauce, 23
Comfort Khichdi with Tomato Onion
      Salad, 85–87
copper, 27, 33, 38, 145, 169, 229
corn and polenta
      about: corn, 121; polenta, 115
      Choctaw Cornbread, 121
      Plant-Infused Polenta with
            Mushroom Medley, 115–17
      Quechua Ceviche, 138–39
crackers, bean, seed, and herb,
      162–63
cucumbers
      about: kimchi with, 175
      The Mesopotamian Pickle,
            178–79
      Tzatziki Sauce, 208–9
cured food. See dried and cured
      foods
curiosity, embracing, 8–10
curry, medicinal yellow, 62–63

D

dandelion
      about: greens (benefits and
            history), 47
      Dandelion Pesto with Pine Nuts,
            204–5
      Garlic Mushroom Dandelion
            Greens, 47
dates
      about, 102
      Date Porridge (Sasqu), 102–3
      other dishes with, 156–57, 165
Dead Sea Scrolls, manna bread
      and, 126
digestion. See also stomach issues,
      settling
      bitters/bitter food for, 33, 237,
            238
      chickpeas for, 61, 81

fennel and, 211
fermented foods and, 122, 172,
      178, 183, 188
garam masala and, 195
gut health, 184, 216 (See also
      bacteria, good, supporting
      gut)
honey and, 129
khichdi/kitchari for, 85
mint and, 145
niacin for, 132
other foods for, 17 (See also
      dandelion; ginger)
sprouted foods and, 126
vermouth as tonic for, 51
warming herbs/spices for, 30,
      149, 241
Divakaruni, Chitra Banerjee, 190
dried and cured foods, 154–69
      about: ancient civilizations and,
            155 (See also specific
            recipes); nutritional
            benefits (See specific
            recipes)
      Aztec Granola Bars, 158–59
      Bean, Seed, and Herb Crackers,
            162–63
      Cacao Bites, 165
      Cree Pemmican, 156–57
      Oven-Dried Kale Chips, 166–67
      Tarahumara Energy Bar, 161
      Timeless Trail Mix, 169
drinks. See fermented foods; teas
      and tonics
Duxelles, 51

E

Egyptian Lotus Root Salad, 101
elderflower, sautéed morels with
      miner's lettuce and, 44–45
Emerson, Ralph Waldo, 76
energy bar, Tarahumara, 161
escarole
      about: benefits and historical
            perspective, 33
      Escarole Linguini, 33–35
Essene Sprouted Wheat Manna
      Bread, 126–27
Ethiopian Injera, 183

F

falafel, 81
farro, in Forest Porcini and Farro, 39–41
Fennel Syrup, 211
fenugreek, about, 192
fermented foods, 170–89. *See also yogurt*
  about: historical perspective, 171 *(See also specific recipes); kimchi, 170, 175; SCOBY and, 184*
  Celtic Druids Honey Mead, 188–89
  Ethiopian Injera, 183
  Herbal Kombucha, 184–85
  Korean Kimchi, 175–77
  The Mesopotamian Pickle, 178–79
  Sacred Sauerkraut, 172–74
  Shamanic Fire Cider, 187
Fertile Crescent Falafel, 81
fiber, 14, 23, 28, 33, 38, 61, 65, 78, 81, 97, 105, 108, 111, 112, 122, 126, 161, 162, 166, 169, 172, 178, 181
figs
  about, 216
  Moraba 'Yeh Anjir (Black Fig Jam), 216–17
fire cider, shamanic, 187
Fire-Roasted Chicken with Maya Adobo Sauce, 135–37
fish. *See seafood*
flu. *See colds and flu, fighting*
folate. *See B vitamins*
Forest Porcini and Farro, 39–41
Four-Herb Brain-Booster Tea, 238–39
French fries, oven-roasted, 105

G

garam masala
  about, 30, 195
  recipe, 195
garlic
  Garlic Mushroom Dandelion Greens, 47

Heal-All Garlic and Olive Oil Infusion, 199–201
ginger
  about: benefits and historical perspective, 18; for simple tea, 221
  Ginger Intention Tonic, 250–52
  Ginger Spinach, 18–19
ginkgo biloba, in Four-Herb Brain-Booster Tea, 238–39
Gladstar, Rosemary, 1, 14, 187
glühwein/glögg or mulled wine, 237
glutamine, about, 66
gluten-free symbol, 11
glycine, about, 66
grains, 106–29. *See also breads and crackers*
  about: asparagus and aborio rice, 118 *(See also rice); barley/ emmer, 102; historical perspective, 107; kamut, 112; oats, 111; polenta, 115*
  Jungle Oatmeal, 111
  Kamut Berry Salad, 112–14
  Plant-Infused Polenta with Mushroom Medley, 115–17
  Roman Honey Cake, 129
  Sasqu (Date Porridge), 102–3
grandparents (Nick and Fran), 3–6, 7, 11
granola
  Aztec Granola Bars, 158–59
  Superfood Yogurt Bowl, 181
greens, 12–35
  about: bitter leaf, 20; cauliflower and, 23; chicory, 24; collard greens and kale, 23; dandelion, 47; escarole, 33; historical and sacred ritual/symbolic perspective, 13; kale, 23, 27; mustard, 17; nutritional benefits *(See specific recipes); saag ("greens") and garam masala, 30; seaweed, 14*
  Escarole Linguini, 33–35
  Garlic Mushroom Dandelion Greens, 47
  Ginger Spinach, 18–19
  Greens in Groundnut Sauce, 23

  Mediterranean Kale Salad, 27
  Mustard Greens Bhutuwa, 17
  Nigerian Bitter Leaf Stew (Ofe Onugbu), 20–21
  Roasted Cauliflower Steaks, 28–29
  Saag Paneer, 30–31
  Seaweed Salad, 14–15
  Summer Chicory Salad, 24–25
guayusa, in Herbal Coffee Alternative, 233
gut health, 61, 216. *See also bacteria, good, supporting gut*

H

Ha Sikil Pa'ak, 202–3
Heal-All Garlic and Olive Oil Infusion, 199–201
heart/cardiovascular disease, reducing risk of, 52, 62, 69, 81, 94, 97, 138, 161, 162, 187, 199, 202, 234
Herbal Coffee Alternative, 233
Herbal Kombucha, 184–85
Herbed Sausage, 146–47
Holiday Mulled Wine, 237
Holy Basil Elixir, 223
honey
  about: benefits and historical perspective, 129; collecting as divine miracle, 225; mulsum wine, 188; tea and, ancient history and, 225
  Celtic Druids Honey Mead, 188–89
  Honey Dijon Dressing, 212–13
  Roman Honey Cake, 129
  Spicy Herbal Honey, 215
hot chocolate, Mayan, 230–31
hummus, Arabian, 90–91
Hussain, Sijdah, 106

I

immune system
  Ayurvedic Immune Booster, 245
  boosting, 6, 24, 44, 47, 48, 58, 61, 74, 149, 172, 178, 181, 187, 199, 245

modulating/regulating, 43, 220, 229, 242
Inca Quinoa Salad, 78–79
inflammation, reducing, 17, 18, 27, 39, 43, 44, 47, 51, 56, 58, 62, 69, 102, 141, 149, 162, 165, 175, 199, 237
Ingerman, Sandra, 1
ingredients, 2–3
ingredients, exploring story of, 8–10. See also specific main ingredients
intention tonic, ginger, 250–52
iron, 14, 38, 65, 78, 89, 108, 126, 169, 229, 249

J

Jarvis, Dr. D. C., 212
Jerusalem artichokes, in Roasted Winter Roots, 97
Jungle Oatmeal, 111

K

kale
    about: benefits of, 27, 166–67; collard greens and kale, 23
    Greens in Groundnut Sauce, 23
    Mediterranean Kale Salad, 27
    Oven-Dried Kale Chips, 166–67
Kamut Berry Salad, 112–14
khichdi with tomato onion salad, 85–87
Kimchi, 170, 175–77
kitchen, making a sacred space, 7
kombucha, herbal, 184–85
Korean Kimchi, 175–77
Kring, Shannon, 135
Kübler-Ross, Elizabeth, 130

L

Lanich-LaBrie, Tara, 58
legumes, seeds, and nuts, 76–91
    about: chickpeas, 81, 90; groundnuts (peanuts), 23; historical reverence for, 77; lentils, 65; pine nuts, 82; quinoa, 78, 89

Arabian Hummus, 90–91
Aztec Granola Bars, 158–59
Bean, Seed, and Herb Crackers, 162–63
Comfort Khichdi with Tomato Onion Salad, 85–87
Cree Pemmican, 156–57
Dandelion Pesto with Pine Nuts, 204–5
Fertile Crescent Falafel, 81
Folk Healing Soup, 56–57
Greens in Groundnut Sauce, 23
Ha Sikil Pa'ak, 202–3
Inca Quinoa Salad, 78–79
Jungle Oatmeal, 111
Lemon Quinoa Salad with Hemp Seed, 89
Pine Nut Pilaf, 82–83
Savory Winter Lentil Soup, 65
Tarahumara Energy Bar, 161
Timeless Trail Mix, 169
Tofu Peanut Dumplings, 153
Traditional Berber Tagine, 61
lentils. See legumes, seeds, and nuts
longevity powder, 229
Longnecker, Callie, 122
lotus root salad, Egyptian, 101
Low Dog, Tieraona, 1, 246

M

maca elixir, 249
magnesium, 27, 38, 65, 66, 81, 89, 126, 145, 158, 169, 180, 202, 229, 249
Maitake Chai, 241
manganese, 27, 81, 158, 169, 208
manna bread, Essene sprouted wheat, 126–27
Māori boil up, traditional, 70–71
Maya Adobo Sauce, 135–37
Mayan Hot Chocolate, 230–31
mead, Celtic druids honey, 188–89
meat. See also dried and cured foods; Medicinal Chinese Dumplings; specific meats
    about: Chimichurri as healing elixir on, 207; consuming as an honor, 131
    Al Kabsa, 132–34

Ancient Herb-Marinated Chicken, 145
Fire-Roasted Chicken with Maya Adobo Sauce, 135–37
Herbed Sausage, 146–47
Nourishing Protein Patties, 142–43
Patarashca: Amazon Roasted Fish, 141
Quechua Ceviche, 138–39
Medicinal Chinese Dumplings, 149–53
    about: benefits and historical perspective, 149
    basic recipe, 149–51
    Dipping Sauce, 149
    Tofu Peanut Dumplings, 153
    Vegetable Dumplings, 153
Medicinal Yellow Curry, 62–63
Mediterranean Kale Salad, 27
Mesopotamian Pickle, 178–79
Moraba 'Yeh Anjir (Black Fig Jam), 216–17
Morning Maca Elixir, 249
mulled wine, 237
mushrooms, 36–53
    about: chanterelle benefits, 43; cremini benefits, 51; historical and functional overview, 37–38; maitake (Hui Shu Hua) benefits, 48; morel benefits and hunts for, 44; porcini benefits, 39; shiitake benefits, 48
    Chaga Latte Elixir, 242–43
    Duxelles, 51
    Forest Porcini and Farro, 39–41
    Garlic Mushroom Dandelion Greens, 47
    Maitake Chai, 241
    Mushroom Tapenade, 52–53
    Plant-Infused Polenta with Mushroom Medley, 115–17
    Reishi Tea, 220–21
    Sautéed Morels with Elderflower and Miner's Lettuce, 44–45
    Savory Seaweed Broth, 58–59
    Simple Chanterelle Mushrooms, 43
    Three Mushroom Stir-Fry, 48–49
mustard, benefits and historical perspective, 17
Mustard Greens Bhutuwa, 17

N

Nam Prik Pau, 196–98
niacin, 38, 132
Nigerian Bitter Leaf Stew (Ofe
   Onugbu), 20–21
Nourishing Bone Broth, 66–67
Nourishing Protein Patties, 142–43
nuts and seeds. *See legumes,
   seeds, and nuts*

O

oatmeal, jungle, 111
Oatstraw Infusion, 234–35
Ofe Onugbu (Nigerian Bitter Leaf
   Stew), 20–21
olives and olive oil, 52–53. *See also
   Heal-All Garlic and Olive Oil
   Infusion*
onions and leeks
   Irish Brotchan Roy Foltchep
      Soup, 69
   Tomato Onion Salad, 86–87
oregano, about, 2, 141
organic, eating, 7
Oven-Dried Kale Chips, 166–67
Oven-Roasted Herb French Fries,
   105

P

parsnips, in Roasted Winter Roots,
   97
pasta, Escarole Linguini, 33–35
Patarashca: Amazon Roasted Fish,
   141
Patel, Mileen, 250
peppers
   Maya Adobo Sauce, 135–37
   Nam Prik Pau, 196–98
pesto, dandelion, 204–5
pickle, Mesopotamian, 178–79
Pine Nut Pilaf, 82–83
Pine Pollen Tea, 229
Plain Jane's restaurant, 3, 90, 212
plant-based recipe symbol, 11
polenta. *See corn and polenta*
Polizzi, Nick and Fran
   (grandparents), 3–6, 7, 11

Polizzi, Peggy (mother), 3, 6, 90
Polizzi, Steve (father), 6
pork
   Herbed Sausage, 146–47
   Medicinal Chinese Dumplings,
      149–53
potassium, 23, 24, 27, 38, 65, 78,
   89, 97, 101, 166, 169, 180
potatoes
   about: benefits and historical
      perspective, 105
   Oven-Roasted Herb French
      Fries, 105
   Q'ero Potato Salad, 98–99
   soup/stew with, 56, 61
   Vegetable Dumplings, 153
praying before meal, 10–11
protein patties, 142–43

Q

Q'ero Potato Salad, 98–99
Q'ero tribe, about, 98
Quechua Ceviche, 138–39
Quechua Yucca Salad, 102–3
quinoa
   about: benefits and historical
      perspective, 78, 89
   Aztec Granola Bars, 158–59
   Lemon Quinoa Salad with Hemp
      Seed, 89
   Pine Nut Pilaf, 82–83

R

Rajneesh, Bhagwan Shree, 218
recipes, criteria for, 2–3. *See also
   specific main ingredients*
Reishi Tea, 220–21
rhodiola tea, Tibetan, 226–27
riboflavin. *See B vitamins*
rice
   about: arborio, 118
   Al Kabsa, 132–34
   Asparagus Risotto, 118–19
   Comfort Khichdi with Tomato
      Onion Salad, 85–87
   Seaweed Salad, 14–15
Roasted Cauliflower Steaks, 28–29
Robbins, Tom, 92
Roman Honey Cake, 129

root vegetables, 92–105. *See also
   potatoes*
   about: beets, 94; benefits and
      historical perspective, 93;
      carrots, 97; Jerusalem
      artichokes, 97; lotus
      root, 101; potatoes, 105;
      rutabagas, 97; turnips, 97;
      well-stocked root cellar,
      99; yucca plant, 102
   Egyptian Lotus Root Salad, 101
   Oven-Roasted Herb French
      Fries, 105
   Q'ero Potato Salad, 98–99
   Quechua Yucca Salad, 102–3
   Roasted Winter Roots, 97
   Summer Borscht, 94–95
rutabagas, in Roasted Winter Roots,
   97

S

Saag Paneer, 30–31
sacred cooking
   about: healing power of food and,
      1–2
   authors' backgrounds and, 1–6
   blessing your food, 10–11
   eating organic and, 7
   embracing curiosity, exploring
      story of ingredients, 8–10
   Grandpa Nick, Grandma Fran
      and, 3–6
   intentions and, 7–8
   making kitchen a sacred space, 7
   philosophy of, 6–11
   seasonal eating and, 8
Sacred Sauerkraut, 172–74
Sacred Science (online community),
   1, 6
saffron, about, 56
salads
   Egyptian Lotus Root Salad, 101
   Inca Quinoa Salad, 78–79
   Kamut Berry Salad, 112–14
   Lemon Quinoa Salad with Hemp
      Seed, 89
   Mediterranean Kale Salad, 27
   Q'ero Potato Salad, 98–99
   Quechua Yucca Salad, 102–3
   Seaweed Salad, 14–15

Summer Chicory Salad, 24–25
Tomato Onion Salad, 86–87
sandwiches. *See Nourishing Protein Patties*
Sasqu (Date Porridge), 102–3
sauces. See spices and sauces
sauerkraut, sacred, 172–74
sausage, herbed, 146–47
Sautéed Morels with Elderflower and Miner's Lettuce, 44–45
Savory Seaweed Broth, 58–59
Savory Winter Lentil Soup, 65
seafood
    about: cooking without any heat, 138; nutritional benefits, 138
    Caribbean Pepperpot Recipe, 73
    Medicinal Chinese Dumplings, 149–53
    Nigerian Bitter Leaf Stew (Ofe Onugbu), 20–21
    Patarashca: Amazon Roasted Fish, 141
    Tom Yum Soup, 74–75
seasonal eating, 8
seaweed
    about: benefits and historical perspective, 14
    Savory Seaweed Broth, 58–59
    Seaweed Salad, 14–15
Shamanic Fire Cider, 187
Simple Chanterelle Mushrooms, 43
Simpson, Louis, 54
soups and stews, 54–75
    about: making, 55
    Caribbean Pepperpot Recipe, 73
    Folk Healing Soup, 56–57
    Irish Brotchan Roy Foltchep Soup, 69
    Medicinal Yellow Curry, 62–63
    Nigerian Bitter Leaf Stew (Ofe Onugbu), 20–21
    Nourishing Bone Broth, 66–67
    Savory Seaweed Broth, 58–59
    Savory Winter Lentil Soup, 65
    Summer Borscht, 94–95
    Tom Yum Soup, 74–75
    Traditional Berber Tagine, 61
    Traditional Māori Puha Boil Up, 70–71
Sourdough Bread, 122–25

spices and sauces
    about: historical importance of spices, 191 (*See also specific spices*)
    Berbere Spice, 192–93
    Chimichurri, 207
    Dandelion Pesto with Pine Nuts, 204–5
    Dipping Sauce, 149
    Fennel Syrup, 211
    Garam Masala, 195
    Groundnut Sauce, 23
    Ha Sikil Pa'ak, 202–3
    Heal-All Garlic and Olive Oil Infusion, 199–201
    Honey Dijon Dressing, 212–13
    Lemon-Garlic Dressing, 27
    Maya Adobo Sauce, 135–37
    Moraba 'Yeh Anjir (Black Fig Jam), 216–17
    Nam Prik Pau, 196–98
    Spicy Herbal Honey, 215
    Tzatziki Sauce, 208–9
Spicy Herbal Honey, 215
spinach
    about: benefits and historical perspective, 30; saag ("greens") and garam masala, 30
    Ginger Spinach, 18–19
    Pine Nut Pilaf, 82–83
    Saag Paneer, 30–31
    Vegetable Dumplings, 153
Standage, Tom, 12
stir-fry, three mushroom, 48–49
stomach issues, settling, 18, 27, 51, 162, 199. *See also digestion*
stroke, reducing risk of, 52, 94, 138
Summer Chicory Salad, 24–25

T

Tannahil, Reay, 154
tapenade, mushroom, 52–53
Tarahumara Energy Bar, 161
taro, in Nigerian Bitter Leaf Stew (Ofe Onugbu), 20–21
teas and tonics, 218–53

    about: almighty honey and, 225; ancient traditions, 219; healing properties, 219 (*See also specific teas*); Rajneesh on, 218; seven super herbs perfect for simple tea, 221
    Ashwagandha Milk, 246–47
    Ayurvedic Immune Booster, 245
    Chaga Latte Elixir, 242–43
    Four-Herb Brain-Booster Tea, 238–39
    Ginger Intention Tonic, 250–52
    Herbal Coffee Alternative, 233
    Holiday Mulled Wine, 237
    Holy Basil Elixir, 223
    Homemade Coconut Milk, 224–25
    Maitake Chai, 241
    Mayan Hot Chocolate, 230–31
    Morning Maca Elixir, 249
    Oatstraw Infusion, 234–35
    Pine Pollen Tea, 229
    Reishi Tea, 220–21
    Tibetan Rhodiola Tea, 226–27
teff, in Ethiopian Injera, 183
Thai chili pepper, Nam Prik Pau, 196–98
The Sacred Science (film), 1–2
thiamine, 162
Three Mushroom Stir-Fry, 48–49
Tibetan Rhodiola Tea, 226–27
Timeless Trail Mix, 169
tofu or seitan
    Medicinal Chinese Dumplings, 149–53
    Tofu Peanut Dumplings, 153
Tom Yum Soup, 74–75
tomatoes
    Ha Sikil Pa'ak, 202–3
    Tomato Onion Salad, 86–87
tonics. *See teas and tonics*

Traditional Chinese Medicine
    on boiling herbs/roots with
        vegetables and meat,
        55
    coconut shavings and, 181
    fennel and, 211
    fenugreek and, 192
    ginger root and, 18
    ginkgo biloba and, 238
    lotus root and, 101
    maitake mushroom (Hui Shu Hua)
        and, 48
    oats balancing hormones,
        stabilizing moods, 111
    reishi and, 220
trail mix, timeless, 169
triglycerides, lowering, 212
tulsi, Holy Basil Elixir, 223
turkey, in Cree Pemmican, 156–57
turmeric, about, 2, 56, 190, 191
turnips, in Roasted Winter Roots,
    97
Tzatziki Sauce, 208–9

V

vegan (plant-based) recipe symbol,
    11
vermouth, about, 51
viruses, fighting, 27, 39, 47, 51, 74,
    141, 187, 199, 245
vitamin A, 23, 24, 27, 33, 61, 145,
    166, 169, 208
vitamin B, 24, 78, 81, 122, 166, 169,
    172, 180, 229, 249
    B1(thiamine), 162
    B2 (riboflavin), 180
    B3 (niacin), 38, 132
    B6, 27, 65, 131
    B9 (folate), 94, 118
    B12, 131, 166, 180
vitamin C, 23, 24, 27, 33, 97, 102,
    166, 169, 172, 208
vitamin D, 138
vitamin E, 78, 81
vitamin K, 23, 24, 27, 33, 145, 169,
    172

W

wheat breads. *See breads and
    crackers*
wine, holiday mulled, 237
wormwood, about, 51

Y

yogurt
    about: benefits and history of,
        180
    Superfood Yogurt Bowl, 181
    Tzatziki Sauce, 208–9
    Yogurt (Laban), 180
yucca root, in Quechua Yucca
    Salad, 102–3

Z

zinc, 38, 81, 89, 126, 145, 169, 229,
    249

ACKNOWLEDGMENTS

First and foremost, thank you to our creative team, including our brilliant writing partner, Amanda Ibey, who is a true master at her craft—without you, this book wouldn't have been possible. Another big shout out to our partner in research and a true mentor in the kitchen, Nick's mom, Peggy Polizzi.

So much gratitude as well to our wonderful contributors—Rosemary Gladstar, Tieraona Low Dog, Tara Lanich-LaBrie, Callie Longenecker, Minaxi Patel, Mileen Patel, and Shannon Kring.

A big hug (and infinite appreciation) to the Hay House family for all of your hard work on this book and for always believing in us.

Lastly, thank you to Nick's grandparents Nick and Fran Polizzi, who taught their children and grandchildren how to cook with love, presence, and a deep reverence for every ingredient we drop into the pot.

ABOUT THE AUTHORS

NICK POLIZZI is the founder of The Sacred Science, director of the feature documentary by the same name, and author of the book based on the film. He is also the host and executive producer of a number of documentary series, including *The Healing Kitchen, Remedy: Ancient Medicine for Modern Illness,* and *Proven: Healing Breakthroughs Backed by Science.* Ever since he cured himself of a debilitating illness using a traditional therapy, he has been traveling the world and documenting forgotten healing methods.

MICHELLE POLIZZI is a ceramic and botanical artist, a published photographer and illustrator, and mother of two big-hearted, earth-loving boys. She is the co-creator of The Sacred Science and creator of Earth Magic, Mother Nature's Guide for Creativity + Wonder. When she isn't creating or playing in nature with her family, you can find Michelle getting her hands dirty nurturing the plants in her herb and dye gardens.

www.thesacredscience.com

A GIFT FROM US TO YOU

Thank you for reading this book from cover to cover! To aid you on your natural healing journey, we are gifting you full access to an exclusive video collection that will show you how to harness the healing power of herbs, spices, and essential oils.

If you enjoyed *The Sacred Cookbook*, this complimentary program will take your culinary experience to the next level!

To watch, visit thesacredscience.com/cookbook-gift.

Hay House Titles of Related Interest

YOU CAN HEAL YOUR LIFE, the movie, starring Louise Hay & Friends
(available as an online streaming video)
www.hayhouse.com/louise-movie

THE SHIFT, the movie,
starring Dr. Wayne W. Dyer
(available as an online streaming video)
www.hayhouse.com/the-shift-movie

* * *

THE FOOD MATTERS COOKBOOK:
A Simple Gluten-Free Guide to Transforming Your Health One Meal at a Time,
by James Colquhoun & Laurentine ten Bosch

GROW A NEW BODY:
How Spirit and Power Plant Nutrients Can Transform Your Health,
by Alberto Villoldo, Ph.D.

JOY'S SIMPLE FOOD REMEDIES:
Tasty Cures for Whatever's Ailing You,
by Joy Bauer

UPGRADE YOUR IMMUNITY WITH HERBS:
Herbal Tonics, Broths, Brews, and Elixirs to Supercharge Your Immune System,
by Dr. Joseph Mercola

All of the above are available at your local bookstore,
or may be ordered by contacting Hay House (see next page).

* * *

We hope you enjoyed this Hay House book. If you'd like to receive our online catalog featuring additional information on Hay House books and products, or if you'd like to find out more about the Hay Foundation, please contact:

Hay House, Inc., P.O. Box 5100, Carlsbad, CA 92018-5100
(760) 431-7695 or (800) 654-5126
(760) 431-6948 (fax) or (800) 650-5115 (fax)
www.hayhouse.com® • www.hayfoundation.org

———

Published in Australia by: Hay House Australia Pty. Ltd.,
18/36 Ralph St., Alexandria NSW 2015
Phone: 612-9669-4299 • *Fax:* 612-9669-4144
www.hayhouse.com.au

Published in the United Kingdom by: Hay House UK, Ltd.,
The Sixth Floor, Watson House, 54 Baker Street, London W1U 7BU
Phone: +44 (0)20 3927 7290 • *Fax:* +44 (0)20 3927 7291
www.hayhouse.co.uk

Published in India by: Hay House Publishers India,
Muskaan Complex, Plot No. 3, B-2, Vasant Kunj, New Delhi 110 070
Phone: 91-11-4176-1620 • *Fax:* 91-11-4176-1630
www.hayhouse.co.in

———

Access New Knowledge.
Anytime. Anywhere.

Learn and evolve at your own pace
with the world's leading experts.

www.hayhouseU.com